Name  ____ Date _____

11 + 18	14 + 9			5 + 9	8 + 2	20 + 6	5 + 20	11 + 7	20 + 19

8 + 12	2 + 18	12 + 8	20 + 2	6 + 14	7 + 2	8 + 3	6 + 18	2 + 8	12 + 6

13 + 20	6 + 9	15 + 8	18 + 7	14 + 18	2 + 10	14 + 11	2 + 4	14 + 6	9 + 3

13 + 12	15 + 2	13 + 13	10 + 2	15 + 6	8 + 5	12 + 2	7 + 10	16 + 7	16 + 13

15 + 14	6 + 2	18 + 6	2 + 7	9 + 6	13 + 10	16 + 16	19 + 3	11 + 3	17 + 2

9 + 7	4 + 15	19 + 13	7 + 13	18 + 17	9 + 8	7 + 18	14 + 17	18 + 3	10 + 11

17 + 9	12 + 5	3 + 17	6 + 4	17 + 7	17 + 6	14 + 16	5 + 6	8 + 20	16 + 9

3 + 19	8 + 9	20 + 20	17 + 8	18 + 9	3 + 11	2 + 3	3 + 15	8 + 16	18 + 15

12 + 7	3 + 7	19 + 5	3 + 12	6 + 7	4 + 20	10 + 7	16 + 5	15 + 10	2 + 15

6 + 16	4 + 4	4 + 18	17 + 12	5 + 10	5 + 11	11 + 12	5 + 5	14 + 13	13 + 5

Name _____ Date _____

13 + 5	14 + 20	12 + 16	14 + 11	5 + 8	9 + 3	19 + 4	10 + 12	14 + 5	11 + 18
19 + 3	12 + 7	15 + 15	15 + 14	19 + 11	8 + 16	17 + 8	14 + 19	19 + 15	18 + 4
16 + 4	12 + 3	11 + 13	8 + 10	8 + 17	6 + 7	19 + 13	4 + 12	2 + 16	16 + 10
4 + 15	13 + 6	15 + 18	2 + 13	12 + 4	6 + 9	16 + 3	8 + 9	5 + 11	4 + 5
11 + 3	3 + 17	6 + 19	14 + 7	5 + 2	6 + 8	11 + 4	16 + 12	15 + 17	8 + 8
20 + 6	9 + 5	20 + 9	16 + 11	13 + 2	5 + 18	7 + 7	18 + 14	3 + 4	7 + 3
13 + 9	4 + 3	3 + 7	8 + 2	3 + 8	19 + 18	16 + 18	13 + 15	8 + 7	11 + 20
20 + 13	20 + 4	4 + 9	4 + 11	18 + 11	15 + 7	19 + 19	3 + 10	11 + 12	10 + 17
12 + 13	20 + 5	4 + 16	8 + 19	6 + 14	17 + 15	9 + 8	18 + 18	17 + 4	9 + 12
11 + 14	17 + 13	18 + 12	12 + 14	18 + 6	13 + 12	3 + 11	3 + 5	20 + 8	2 + 7

Name _____   Date _____

7 + 18	13 + 18	14 + 17	19 + 19	9 + 5	10 + 8	2 + 19	15 + 4	3 + 8	10 + 4
3 + 13	7 + 5	7 + 14	8 + 6	12 + 7	6 + 5	13 + 11	20 + 10	7 + 12	6 + 17
3 + 4	11 + 11	2 + 5	13 + 8	17 + 3	16 + 5	20 + 11	19 + 20	4 + 17	11 + 13
11 + 4	15 + 9	5 + 3	10 + 9	8 + 17	20 + 13	3 + 6	10 + 11	14 + 16	9 + 12
17 + 2	20 + 7	7 + 19	11 + 2	11 + 19	4 + 6	20 + 15	19 + 14	6 + 12	11 + 18
10 + 5	5 + 8	14 + 19	9 + 20	18 + 3	3 + 10	3 + 14	17 + 4	11 + 15	15 + 15
8 + 9	20 + 8	17 + 5	9 + 2	17 + 10	16 + 15	12 + 8	14 + 8	20 + 2	7 + 3
15 + 16	10 + 15	18 + 4	9 + 8	10 + 12	3 + 3	18 + 13	11 + 9	10 + 7	5 + 4
9 + 13	5 + 9	12 + 14	16 + 9	6 + 11	2 + 17	12 + 6	18 + 17	2 + 12	3 + 7
9 + 17	17 + 6	19 + 2	5 + 14	15 + 18	3 + 2	15 + 2	10 + 17	2 + 11	5 + 13

Name _____   Date _____

13 + 16	7 + 11	11 + 10	17 + 13	13 + 9	6 + 10	3 + 12	17 + 4	6 + 7	14 + 15
14 + 14	3 + 11	8 + 2	7 + 14	11 + 17	8 + 20	2 + 13	10 + 17	5 + 14	19 + 6
19 + 19	13 + 7	12 + 4	12 + 19	9 + 9	5 + 17	18 + 9	16 + 2	18 + 2	16 + 5
20 + 9	8 + 3	19 + 8	9 + 10	9 + 3	14 + 4	15 + 5	5 + 11	19 + 15	19 + 2
15 + 15	2 + 17	9 + 5	7 + 18	19 + 4	10 + 16	19 + 10	3 + 18	6 + 18	7 + 5
15 + 20	10 + 2	4 + 12	17 + 20	8 + 12	20 + 13	18 + 3	4 + 9	18 + 6	3 + 17
10 + 3	5 + 18	5 + 6	11 + 11	9 + 11	10 + 6	8 + 9	12 + 13	9 + 13	2 + 9
2 + 4	13 + 8	4 + 11	13 + 3	12 + 8	7 + 7	5 + 13	19 + 18	3 + 10	3 + 4
16 + 6	15 + 17	5 + 2	18 + 14	3 + 7	14 + 2	9 + 20	5 + 4	18 + 10	11 + 13
3 + 8	13 + 19	3 + 19	13 + 13	20 + 6	7 + 8	8 + 14	14 + 5	17 + 14	3 + 2

Name _____   Date _____

6 + 8	16 + 16	6 + 6	5 + 13	12 + 16	5 + 9	15 + 6	4 + 5	2 + 14	8 + 15
17 + 11	3 + 14	14 + 16	17 + 10	4 + 6	11 + 9	4 + 17	13 + 3	9 + 5	12 + 5
17 + 4	9 + 6	12 + 12	20 + 19	13 + 18	5 + 10	13 + 10	16 + 3	2 + 19	19 + 6
10 + 12	20 + 4	13 + 14	4 + 12	16 + 12	8 + 14	17 + 13	6 + 16	4 + 8	3 + 16
12 + 3	2 + 18	3 + 2	20 + 6	19 + 11	14 + 20	6 + 11	9 + 2	6 + 3	7 + 10
17 + 3	19 + 19	3 + 11	14 + 10	2 + 10	6 + 5	2 + 16	13 + 9	17 + 15	7 + 5
7 + 4	19 + 3	15 + 13	3 + 18	8 + 6	7 + 16	15 + 8	8 + 12	19 + 8	7 + 2
10 + 6	11 + 19	10 + 4	20 + 13	9 + 19	3 + 5	16 + 20	19 + 15	18 + 17	8 + 3
9 + 12	3 + 19	9 + 10	20 + 9	16 + 17	3 + 15	15 + 11	9 + 3	20 + 8	11 + 14
11 + 8	16 + 4	18 + 15	19 + 12	11 + 18	7 + 15	11 + 7	5 + 16	15 + 12	15 + 19

Name _____   Date _____

7 + 9	16 + 8	9 + 5	11 + 3	13 + 9	4 + 12	10 + 8	4 + 5	17 + 6	7 + 16
5 + 3	10 + 11	9 + 7	3 + 6	8 + 17	14 + 19	2 + 10	20 + 5	13 + 5	10 + 7
4 + 11	12 + 17	13 + 7	6 + 2	3 + 7	4 + 16	20 + 10	14 + 11	10 + 14	11 + 7
19 + 3	19 + 14	18 + 4	13 + 13	14 + 12	19 + 4	11 + 5	5 + 2	7 + 17	17 + 18
3 + 19	2 + 20	12 + 9	19 + 7	9 + 6	8 + 8	2 + 4	2 + 18	7 + 14	5 + 19
7 + 11	20 + 3	18 + 18	9 + 20	20 + 18	20 + 19	2 + 14	11 + 19	5 + 11	4 + 18
18 + 13	13 + 19	2 + 9	8 + 7	2 + 6	12 + 14	20 + 8	12 + 13	11 + 13	15 + 20
6 + 12	14 + 9	16 + 12	6 + 15	19 + 6	13 + 2	11 + 2	4 + 13	11 + 12	18 + 16
4 + 14	18 + 11	7 + 18	14 + 4	8 + 2	8 + 10	7 + 19	18 + 6	14 + 14	20 + 14
18 + 10	15 + 11	9 + 16	8 + 5	14 + 17	12 + 2	10 + 19	19 + 19	18 + 17	15 + 12

13 + 7	16 + 4	11 + 13	11 + 7	9 + 16	9 + 19	4 + 3	14 + 5	15 + 12	3 + 11
6 + 12	20 + 18	9 + 10	16 + 7	17 + 9	12 + 6	2 + 3	16 + 9	11 + 14	5 + 4
3 + 13	7 + 2	12 + 17	2 + 18	13 + 13	4 + 14	6 + 9	13 + 2	2 + 19	2 + 16
10 + 19	6 + 8	17 + 14	18 + 2	13 + 9	5 + 17	14 + 15	6 + 10	2 + 2	3 + 8
20 + 3	8 + 6	8 + 18	4 + 5	11 + 20	11 + 16	6 + 6	8 + 11	9 + 7	5 + 14
7 + 17	3 + 10	12 + 5	13 + 8	8 + 15	17 + 2	9 + 11	13 + 3	13 + 4	19 + 10
8 + 19	3 + 5	13 + 14	9 + 9	10 + 5	18 + 10	15 + 2	8 + 5	14 + 13	14 + 18
9 + 18	10 + 10	9 + 2	18 + 6	3 + 7	6 + 19	18 + 12	18 + 19	6 + 14	8 + 7
6 + 5	8 + 14	17 + 15	6 + 15	8 + 4	20 + 16	18 + 17	4 + 4	9 + 3	13 + 15
15 + 9	7 + 7	2 + 14	8 + 9	18 + 16	7 + 10	4 + 2	18 + 4	4 + 12	6 + 2

6 + 13	9 + 11	2 + 4	19 + 15	12 + 5	12 + 19	11 + 6	5 + 11	11 + 5	4 + 2
20 + 2	16 + 9	7 + 5	15 + 5	20 + 10	9 + 19	10 + 10	19 + 5	12 + 18	10 + 13
5 + 4	14 + 2	19 + 13	13 + 12	15 + 12	17 + 17	14 + 19	20 + 3	18 + 13	3 + 20
20 + 16	5 + 5	7 + 13	15 + 17	20 + 18	11 + 10	12 + 11	15 + 2	5 + 10	5 + 19
2 + 7	2 + 20	18 + 4	11 + 7	11 + 4	17 + 8	2 + 11	8 + 12	19 + 11	14 + 13
4 + 17	18 + 6	3 + 14	8 + 10	7 + 4	13 + 3	11 + 16	20 + 14	18 + 7	19 + 9
4 + 3	15 + 4	4 + 19	13 + 17	19 + 3	4 + 8	16 + 14	6 + 20	8 + 2	16 + 3
7 + 8	7 + 9	9 + 6	7 + 2	2 + 14	10 + 4	3 + 17	4 + 7	5 + 7	14 + 14
17 + 18	9 + 16	17 + 7	10 + 17	14 + 16	20 + 19	14 + 6	2 + 10	20 + 15	4 + 6
20 + 7	14 + 17	2 + 9	17 + 5	10 + 7	16 + 7	18 + 19	6 + 9	6 + 12	12 + 9

Name _____   Date _____

4 + 20	13 + 18	20 + 9	2 + 3	16 + 12	18 + 2	6 + 5	11 + 4	19 + 3	16 + 14
8 + 20	4 + 16	11 + 8	19 + 8	2 + 6	8 + 3	3 + 3	6 + 19	6 + 6	3 + 4
20 + 4	14 + 14	7 + 7	6 + 10	20 + 16	13 + 3	9 + 10	13 + 4	18 + 11	9 + 12
9 + 4	2 + 16	8 + 10	20 + 5	11 + 6	12 + 5	17 + 20	19 + 2	2 + 14	15 + 13
15 + 7	4 + 15	19 + 19	7 + 20	3 + 14	3 + 8	18 + 12	14 + 10	14 + 16	4 + 17
12 + 17	12 + 3	3 + 12	20 + 8	18 + 7	4 + 12	12 + 11	10 + 2	16 + 5	14 + 8
16 + 11	9 + 15	6 + 2	15 + 11	2 + 19	20 + 2	4 + 9	6 + 12	18 + 14	13 + 6
5 + 2	20 + 20	6 + 11	15 + 9	6 + 3	2 + 9	17 + 9	11 + 14	2 + 17	17 + 10
16 + 9	12 + 4	20 + 17	15 + 20	15 + 4	3 + 7	3 + 13	14 + 6	19 + 9	16 + 17
8 + 5	4 + 7	4 + 14	15 + 2	16 + 20	9 + 3	17 + 13	7 + 12	18 + 19	18 + 6

Name _____   Date _____

2 + 7	18 + 5	19 + 2	20 + 18	15 + 13	16 + 12	3 + 10	10 + 7	5 + 9	14 + 6
8 + 16	10 + 11	10 + 6	4 + 4	5 + 5	11 + 11	20 + 5	15 + 11	6 + 7	2 + 5
17 + 16	19 + 12	17 + 11	12 + 18	9 + 20	20 + 14	2 + 11	7 + 18	19 + 4	13 + 2
9 + 12	4 + 15	10 + 12	12 + 16	6 + 8	9 + 19	9 + 5	8 + 6	6 + 12	9 + 3
4 + 5	2 + 15	14 + 3	6 + 20	14 + 16	7 + 16	13 + 12	4 + 14	9 + 15	13 + 6
14 + 2	15 + 15	5 + 2	13 + 9	15 + 16	12 + 14	7 + 14	8 + 2	20 + 17	16 + 14
16 + 15	11 + 12	11 + 2	5 + 15	4 + 8	7 + 2	19 + 14	8 + 19	8 + 7	14 + 10
8 + 12	20 + 19	16 + 9	18 + 10	3 + 5	3 + 17	20 + 3	19 + 8	6 + 11	6 + 19
5 + 17	20 + 10	14 + 9	18 + 9	17 + 6	9 + 11	3 + 20	15 + 2	13 + 14	16 + 11
17 + 9	20 + 8	11 + 6	15 + 10	18 + 11	17 + 17	4 + 19	19 + 13	17 + 5	4 + 16

Name _____ Date _____

18 + 13	7 + 7	14 + 19	18 + 19	3 + 7	19 + 7	7 + 6	13 + 5	13 + 18	17 + 17
7 + 4	17 + 10	12 + 6	17 + 3	17 + 19	5 + 11	13 + 14	8 + 8	14 + 6	12 + 7
18 + 3	11 + 8	17 + 4	18 + 8	19 + 8	5 + 2	9 + 20	10 + 2	13 + 17	19 + 18
14 + 17	5 + 4	11 + 15	20 + 11	12 + 19	18 + 15	19 + 15	17 + 2	17 + 18	9 + 5
11 + 17	10 + 5	9 + 7	6 + 4	11 + 12	5 + 5	14 + 8	2 + 19	20 + 5	12 + 12
2 + 13	12 + 11	10 + 11	4 + 19	17 + 8	8 + 12	17 + 9	10 + 3	9 + 2	12 + 3
11 + 7	3 + 3	2 + 15	9 + 8	5 + 10	19 + 11	10 + 8	2 + 3	17 + 5	6 + 6
10 + 7	10 + 12	15 + 9	16 + 8	17 + 15	16 + 6	11 + 10	13 + 6	12 + 9	10 + 9
20 + 15	8 + 20	7 + 8	19 + 6	16 + 12	16 + 4	16 + 15	11 + 13	3 + 16	14 + 9
12 + 13	16 + 16	17 + 20	8 + 7	7 + 16	12 + 10	18 + 12	13 + 9	3 + 19	13 + 2

9 + 2	14 + 7	13 + 5	19 + 6	10 + 13	14 + 6	19 + 16	3 + 15	6 + 10	9 + 17
17 + 8	3 + 12	6 + 19	5 + 12	19 + 3	17 + 3	17 + 15	4 + 6	8 + 15	8 + 7
4 + 12	15 + 14	15 + 3	8 + 16	4 + 3	8 + 19	12 + 15	4 + 19	12 + 2	12 + 5
19 + 11	3 + 8	2 + 20	4 + 8	10 + 6	16 + 4	9 + 10	4 + 7	2 + 18	9 + 4
6 + 3	12 + 17	5 + 13	15 + 11	7 + 14	8 + 2	20 + 14	11 + 20	13 + 13	12 + 7
18 + 5	15 + 8	16 + 16	18 + 13	16 + 17	20 + 13	2 + 12	10 + 15	5 + 2	3 + 7
6 + 17	12 + 18	8 + 8	2 + 4	13 + 9	3 + 11	18 + 9	10 + 2	17 + 10	12 + 8
16 + 2	20 + 11	14 + 17	8 + 13	19 + 9	4 + 13	14 + 9	18 + 3	13 + 10	2 + 8
6 + 12	14 + 14	3 + 20	17 + 9	12 + 13	3 + 19	20 + 12	19 + 15	13 + 3	14 + 18
14 + 3	7 + 19	7 + 15	16 + 6	9 + 9	7 + 11	10 + 9	16 + 7	18 + 12	12 + 10

Name _____ Date _____

5 + 2	20 + 11	3 + 9	17 + 14	11 + 10	2 + 8	5 + 11	20 + 14	19 + 2	11 + 18
4 + 15	5 + 18	4 + 12	13 + 18	7 + 16	10 + 12	8 + 20	13 + 3	16 + 14	20 + 12
9 + 12	17 + 7	16 + 8	11 + 13	9 + 4	12 + 6	7 + 9	14 + 5	10 + 11	2 + 7
4 + 19	2 + 20	12 + 2	12 + 9	14 + 15	8 + 4	20 + 19	18 + 7	17 + 3	12 + 7
7 + 10	17 + 5	3 + 12	14 + 16	11 + 8	11 + 9	17 + 10	5 + 6	15 + 2	17 + 9
17 + 4	20 + 18	3 + 6	15 + 7	9 + 3	19 + 10	8 + 8	6 + 2	10 + 15	19 + 16
18 + 8	13 + 6	10 + 9	9 + 14	8 + 11	2 + 14	7 + 4	19 + 5	20 + 17	2 + 18
14 + 7	2 + 13	3 + 14	12 + 16	6 + 18	10 + 8	7 + 6	6 + 7	11 + 5	17 + 12
4 + 10	11 + 14	4 + 4	5 + 5	8 + 10	18 + 15	16 + 15	12 + 15	15 + 9	17 + 6
13 + 2	19 + 8	11 + 2	17 + 11	5 + 10	15 + 18	16 + 11	2 + 11	15 + 12	20 + 10

Name _____ Date _____

10 + 5	20 + 6	2 + 20	18 + 4	8 + 11	14 + 13	12 + 2	7 + 2	10 + 9	2 + 7
7 + 3	18 + 13	18 + 18	10 + 8	20 + 2	5 + 20	18 + 15	10 + 4	11 + 4	20 + 11
17 + 13	5 + 19	9 + 9	16 + 11	19 + 8	6 + 7	5 + 14	9 + 12	19 + 2	16 + 5
10 + 15	12 + 10	2 + 16	13 + 3	3 + 4	9 + 6	17 + 11	13 + 4	15 + 4	3 + 19
14 + 15	4 + 5	8 + 8	16 + 8	4 + 2	4 + 17	11 + 6	3 + 5	16 + 17	18 + 20
17 + 4	12 + 18	19 + 11	15 + 18	2 + 9	16 + 6	14 + 14	6 + 16	10 + 2	14 + 20
19 + 14	17 + 18	13 + 5	12 + 17	18 + 19	5 + 6	11 + 3	7 + 5	19 + 18	15 + 6
15 + 7	7 + 16	7 + 20	14 + 16	8 + 13	5 + 13	9 + 2	16 + 4	2 + 2	6 + 2
10 + 7	5 + 2	19 + 3	12 + 14	18 + 5	9 + 15	7 + 6	19 + 4	13 + 10	5 + 11
19 + 6	2 + 8	17 + 20	10 + 3	15 + 2	3 + 18	13 + 9	7 + 7	12 + 4	12 + 6

17 + 11	13 + 8	6 + 17	7 + 10	14 + 6	9 + 17	3 + 4	6 + 10	9 + 7	11 + 6
4 + 17	3 + 10	19 + 17	16 + 13	7 + 7	5 + 13	16 + 9	18 + 8	7 + 3	19 + 10
11 + 8	18 + 20	10 + 2	20 + 5	17 + 8	18 + 11	15 + 11	19 + 5	12 + 3	10 + 8
10 + 5	15 + 13	6 + 14	14 + 19	19 + 12	19 + 14	15 + 12	5 + 11	13 + 12	16 + 6
18 + 9	13 + 5	7 + 13	19 + 7	2 + 11	14 + 7	14 + 20	12 + 14	5 + 3	8 + 9
12 + 6	14 + 9	10 + 9	17 + 5	17 + 7	8 + 19	7 + 11	15 + 6	18 + 16	18 + 10
18 + 5	17 + 3	19 + 6	16 + 8	17 + 19	20 + 7	7 + 18	17 + 18	10 + 18	12 + 20
7 + 19	6 + 6	10 + 11	7 + 14	8 + 7	18 + 7	5 + 12	7 + 20	10 + 3	19 + 8
13 + 17	16 + 3	8 + 2	17 + 12	17 + 6	11 + 2	7 + 15	8 + 16	16 + 17	4 + 10
15 + 2	16 + 12	11 + 17	4 + 20	19 + 9	13 + 3	12 + 8	7 + 8	19 + 3	14 + 18

Name _____   Date _____

6 + 19	8 + 7	4 + 12	18 + 8	4 + 3	16 + 7	6 + 18	19 + 4	2 + 11	18 + 18
12 + 18	8 + 20	5 + 3	13 + 13	16 + 13	15 + 17	10 + 9	10 + 6	18 + 9	6 + 2
18 + 3	17 + 5	2 + 13	13 + 20	20 + 2	8 + 15	18 + 15	10 + 16	17 + 15	10 + 12
11 + 12	7 + 3	4 + 2	15 + 8	9 + 9	7 + 5	3 + 12	14 + 13	13 + 14	5 + 6
10 + 14	7 + 7	4 + 4	14 + 12	11 + 19	9 + 19	20 + 8	12 + 20	19 + 5	11 + 10
4 + 9	6 + 8	12 + 11	7 + 8	19 + 19	9 + 20	19 + 8	11 + 7	4 + 18	9 + 14
18 + 17	13 + 16	10 + 15	9 + 2	19 + 12	11 + 20	14 + 8	17 + 7	11 + 9	11 + 4
4 + 16	11 + 14	2 + 10	7 + 9	16 + 6	19 + 11	7 + 14	16 + 19	15 + 12	7 + 4
19 + 7	6 + 5	15 + 4	5 + 19	4 + 10	13 + 4	11 + 3	3 + 15	5 + 14	6 + 12
12 + 2	14 + 7	2 + 9	4 + 19	2 + 6	7 + 16	17 + 8	19 + 20	16 + 8	7 + 11

Name _____ Date _____

3 + 5	18 + 4	3 + 17	12 + 10	9 + 16	16 + 5	12 + 11	15 + 17	13 + 5	3 + 20
9 + 9	6 + 6	11 + 2	2 + 11	2 + 6	6 + 5	17 + 16	18 + 9	17 + 9	2 + 12
19 + 10	8 + 15	17 + 3	10 + 5	19 + 3	7 + 9	15 + 9	4 + 9	13 + 3	10 + 11
9 + 6	19 + 16	17 + 13	20 + 20	6 + 17	11 + 8	10 + 3	10 + 20	15 + 6	6 + 20
8 + 10	17 + 4	7 + 10	2 + 3	20 + 9	12 + 20	4 + 2	8 + 16	4 + 16	16 + 6
13 + 2	8 + 6	13 + 18	18 + 19	18 + 11	3 + 19	19 + 20	11 + 14	11 + 19	8 + 12
20 + 8	5 + 2	6 + 7	2 + 15	18 + 14	8 + 19	2 + 19	5 + 7	17 + 17	2 + 9
9 + 3	8 + 14	16 + 4	15 + 10	14 + 11	3 + 13	20 + 15	20 + 11	12 + 4	6 + 14
7 + 16	10 + 8	5 + 12	20 + 12	15 + 4	12 + 18	10 + 19	9 + 2	5 + 6	20 + 19
2 + 13	6 + 19	9 + 7	13 + 13	18 + 3	10 + 7	14 + 5	11 + 13	9 + 13	15 + 18

4 + 3	14 + 4	8 + 6	7 + 13	15 + 15	4 + 7	15 + 6	4 + 19	19 + 18	3 + 11
12 + 3	20 + 14	15 + 17	9 + 18	9 + 4	13 + 3	8 + 4	14 + 7	12 + 8	3 + 9
9 + 16	8 + 8	12 + 14	10 + 4	18 + 18	10 + 9	13 + 2	19 + 3	16 + 6	12 + 17
3 + 20	5 + 3	6 + 9	10 + 2	20 + 18	20 + 3	5 + 16	13 + 6	20 + 4	9 + 10
3 + 3	9 + 6	4 + 9	6 + 15	16 + 2	9 + 14	7 + 10	12 + 5	10 + 10	9 + 20
8 + 2	15 + 20	3 + 13	6 + 16	8 + 19	18 + 16	16 + 19	15 + 7	17 + 20	18 + 13
17 + 17	10 + 6	10 + 8	15 + 9	2 + 16	2 + 11	14 + 2	16 + 3	19 + 6	9 + 3
8 + 11	5 + 18	2 + 6	3 + 7	19 + 15	18 + 17	2 + 13	11 + 16	9 + 19	17 + 12
12 + 11	17 + 4	7 + 8	14 + 6	6 + 2	12 + 20	19 + 4	12 + 4	20 + 11	2 + 20
6 + 14	14 + 3	16 + 10	4 + 12	20 + 12	4 + 2	17 + 8	13 + 15	19 + 2	6 + 19

Name _____ Date _____

10 + 15	20 + 11	9 + 10	20 + 5	7 + 5	15 + 14	9 + 4	19 + 17	20 + 14	10 + 20
13 + 17	17 + 12	8 + 15	13 + 19	17 + 17	4 + 4	3 + 19	9 + 12	17 + 7	15 + 15
8 + 5	18 + 10	9 + 13	11 + 3	20 + 17	12 + 8	11 + 8	20 + 12	5 + 9	19 + 16
6 + 9	15 + 12	12 + 20	3 + 4	12 + 15	10 + 8	15 + 18	3 + 15	5 + 20	20 + 8
17 + 2	6 + 3	2 + 5	3 + 5	4 + 20	9 + 11	20 + 15	10 + 16	13 + 9	16 + 20
13 + 20	18 + 20	4 + 8	6 + 20	15 + 3	20 + 10	13 + 6	11 + 16	5 + 5	12 + 14
16 + 5	15 + 13	16 + 8	3 + 6	7 + 2	3 + 8	6 + 5	4 + 12	12 + 11	4 + 7
10 + 2	3 + 2	6 + 6	2 + 7	17 + 6	14 + 19	12 + 17	18 + 12	17 + 15	20 + 6
14 + 10	20 + 20	3 + 17	9 + 9	8 + 8	6 + 14	15 + 8	18 + 5	7 + 15	14 + 16
10 + 7	18 + 6	20 + 16	3 + 10	14 + 14	19 + 11	8 + 17	2 + 9	6 + 12	10 + 4

Name _____ Date _____

2 + 5	3 + 19	9 + 7	17 + 7	5 + 12	19 + 6	9 + 14	12 + 3	15 + 14	9 + 5
10 + 19	11 + 11	16 + 8	13 + 16	4 + 17	9 + 3	18 + 3	17 + 3	14 + 17	19 + 3
17 + 16	15 + 17	19 + 2	20 + 5	2 + 9	7 + 5	17 + 10	8 + 15	6 + 15	5 + 16
6 + 19	17 + 15	15 + 16	10 + 13	2 + 18	7 + 6	4 + 7	17 + 17	17 + 8	13 + 5
8 + 6	2 + 12	12 + 11	2 + 20	5 + 14	10 + 10	3 + 13	14 + 19	8 + 10	3 + 8
3 + 7	16 + 6	19 + 5	14 + 3	15 + 12	4 + 15	13 + 9	10 + 17	7 + 8	4 + 18
20 + 15	20 + 18	13 + 10	10 + 9	10 + 5	5 + 7	20 + 7	9 + 16	17 + 4	2 + 13
11 + 8	19 + 11	8 + 7	9 + 20	16 + 19	13 + 6	16 + 7	17 + 11	11 + 14	3 + 4
20 + 20	4 + 11	4 + 8	13 + 4	14 + 13	16 + 18	7 + 16	20 + 19	18 + 14	8 + 17
12 + 12	12 + 8	9 + 2	19 + 12	19 + 4	12 + 10	14 + 20	4 + 14	6 + 14	18 + 15

Name _____ Date _____

20 + 16	14 + 7	11 + 9	10 + 3	18 + 13	4 + 10	10 + 18	9 + 9	12 + 8	13 + 3
5 + 8	18 + 3	5 + 10	6 + 12	2 + 17	3 + 6	3 + 18	3 + 4	11 + 7	10 + 15
15 + 17	14 + 4	11 + 8	10 + 16	3 + 2	15 + 19	6 + 20	20 + 15	14 + 6	19 + 10
13 + 9	2 + 18	20 + 7	20 + 6	11 + 11	17 + 15	2 + 5	2 + 14	11 + 4	18 + 5
13 + 17	7 + 7	17 + 9	7 + 13	20 + 12	11 + 5	3 + 3	14 + 3	14 + 15	8 + 6
8 + 2	12 + 18	20 + 17	13 + 5	16 + 15	16 + 5	9 + 16	3 + 8	5 + 9	17 + 6
19 + 7	4 + 12	9 + 12	9 + 4	9 + 15	13 + 14	17 + 8	19 + 18	19 + 13	17 + 10
14 + 16	13 + 18	2 + 11	8 + 5	7 + 4	11 + 3	19 + 3	18 + 12	3 + 14	4 + 3
6 + 2	3 + 7	11 + 20	8 + 19	2 + 7	2 + 9	6 + 19	6 + 7	13 + 13	15 + 3
20 + 9	15 + 15	17 + 20	10 + 13	12 + 14	9 + 11	7 + 11	12 + 3	20 + 5	14 + 8

7 + 3	7 + 7	10 + 17	2 + 6	15 + 17	12 + 10	5 + 6	10 + 18	17 + 15	11 + 3
12 + 12	2 + 4	16 + 14	12 + 6	5 + 3	3 + 8	9 + 10	10 + 4	15 + 19	6 + 5
3 + 3	11 + 10	9 + 4	7 + 2	17 + 3	10 + 11	2 + 15	11 + 5	5 + 13	13 + 5
18 + 6	14 + 16	19 + 10	8 + 13	15 + 10	8 + 5	11 + 7	13 + 18	10 + 5	12 + 19
11 + 15	3 + 2	16 + 18	2 + 7	7 + 13	3 + 5	11 + 8	17 + 2	6 + 9	18 + 14
10 + 3	16 + 11	14 + 10	11 + 18	6 + 11	3 + 13	12 + 17	16 + 15	19 + 8	13 + 16
11 + 17	8 + 17	5 + 9	19 + 18	11 + 14	3 + 10	19 + 17	20 + 7	5 + 8	9 + 16
9 + 18	6 + 7	14 + 12	12 + 5	15 + 9	9 + 7	15 + 8	12 + 14	6 + 19	2 + 10
5 + 16	19 + 6	17 + 12	2 + 18	13 + 11	5 + 10	2 + 9	19 + 11	7 + 14	13 + 19
15 + 15	13 + 14	18 + 7	20 + 10	6 + 16	2 + 14	15 + 5	10 + 6	9 + 13	13 + 8

Name _____ Date _____

2 + 15	20 + 13	7 + 15	12 + 3	18 + 18	14 + 2	2 + 14	16 + 13	8 + 10	10 + 8
4 + 18	10 + 16	19 + 16	3 + 9	9 + 10	7 + 7	10 + 2	12 + 6	12 + 13	18 + 15
5 + 4	17 + 12	12 + 18	14 + 9	4 + 20	14 + 11	13 + 15	3 + 17	3 + 2	19 + 17
13 + 4	14 + 20	16 + 5	18 + 14	13 + 6	17 + 3	9 + 12	20 + 2	7 + 18	5 + 9
9 + 19	2 + 12	8 + 2	8 + 5	7 + 8	4 + 14	20 + 9	15 + 6	8 + 6	10 + 12
5 + 18	10 + 5	2 + 16	11 + 5	8 + 14	18 + 11	7 + 3	12 + 17	3 + 14	18 + 3
3 + 7	2 + 7	9 + 2	12 + 16	5 + 11	4 + 10	11 + 6	20 + 19	20 + 10	13 + 16
17 + 2	15 + 7	15 + 18	3 + 6	9 + 4	18 + 2	8 + 7	11 + 19	10 + 11	12 + 5
6 + 2	17 + 11	11 + 12	15 + 14	14 + 13	14 + 16	6 + 17	16 + 2	18 + 10	9 + 6
2 + 20	19 + 14	10 + 10	5 + 6	9 + 8	16 + 15	13 + 13	18 + 7	5 + 2	15 + 2

| 18 | 19 | 16 | 21 | 12 | 11 | 17 | 16 | 22 | 10 |
| - 6 | -12 | -12 | -12 | - 3 | - 8 | -11 | - 8 | -10 | - 6 |

| 7 | 8 | 12 | 12 | 7 | 15 | 15 | 14 | 20 | 19 |
| - 3 | - 3 | - 6 | - 9 | - 4 | -12 | - 8 | -10 | -10 | - 9 |

| 11 | 21 | 12 | 18 | 13 | 15 | 23 | 20 | 12 | 18 |
| - 5 | - 9 | - 7 | - 9 | - 8 | - 6 | -11 | - 8 | - 5 | -12 |

| 21 | 14 | 14 | 17 | 15 | 12 | 8 | 20 | 9 | 13 |
| -10 | - 4 | - 8 | - 6 | -10 | - 4 | - 4 | - 9 | - 4 | - 5 |

| 13 | 10 | 17 | 16 | 17 | 13 | 18 | 11 | 14 | 17 |
| -10 | - 3 | - 8 | - 5 | - 7 | - 9 | -11 | - 7 | - 9 | -12 |

| 14 | 15 | 21 | 15 | 18 | 12 | 20 | 17 | 11 | 11 |
| - 3 | - 3 | -11 | - 4 | -10 | - 8 | -11 | -10 | - 3 | - 4 |

| 16 | 13 | 16 | 10 | 24 | 18 | 23 | 16 | 11 | 14 |
| -11 | - 3 | - 6 | - 4 | -12 | - 7 | -12 | -10 | - 6 | -11 |

| 6 | 19 | 20 | 13 | 9 | 9 | 16 | 9 | 18 | 10 |
| - 3 | -10 | -12 | - 6 | - 5 | - 6 | - 9 | - 3 | - 8 | - 7 |

| 8 | 17 | 14 | 14 | 15 | 13 | 19 | 14 | 15 | 15 |
| - 5 | - 5 | - 7 | - 6 | - 5 | - 4 | - 7 | - 5 | - 9 | - 7 |

| 19 | 19 | 16 | 22 | 16 | 22 | 13 | 15 | 10 | 17 |
| -11 | - 8 | - 7 | -12 | - 4 | -11 | - 7 | -11 | - 5 | - 9 |

Name _____ Date _____

12 - 6	16 -11	18 - 6	21 -12	19 - 9	12 - 8	19 -12	13 - 6	10 - 6	7 - 3
11 - 8	20 -12	13 - 3	17 - 9	13 -10	18 - 7	17 - 8	21 -10	8 - 5	8 - 4
15 - 7	16 -10	18 -11	13 - 7	14 - 6	13 - 9	14 - 7	23 -12	18 - 9	9 - 3
11 - 3	19 -10	18 -10	24 -12	18 -12	12 - 9	11 - 7	7 - 4	10 - 4	13 - 5
14 - 5	14 - 9	16 - 6	19 - 8	9 - 6	11 - 6	15 - 5	18 - 8	15 - 8	16 - 4
19 -11	17 - 7	13 - 4	17 -12	21 - 9	10 - 7	13 - 8	12 - 4	22 -12	11 - 5
21 -11	9 - 4	10 - 5	16 - 7	14 - 4	10 - 3	22 -11	19 - 7	22 -10	14 - 3
20 -11	17 -10	15 -10	12 - 5	23 -11	20 - 9	20 -10	17 - 6	6 - 3	15 - 3
14 -10	12 - 7	9 - 5	14 - 8	17 -11	8 - 3	17 - 5	14 -11	11 - 4	15 - 4
20 - 8	12 - 3	15 - 6	16 -12	16 - 8	15 -11	15 - 9	16 - 5	16 - 9	15 -12

Name _____ Date _____

17 - 9	8 - 5	14 - 8	7 - 4	14 - 9	20 - 8	13 - 5	11 - 5	15 - 10	15 - 11
8 - 3	17 - 8	10 - 6	14 - 7	15 - 9	19 - 10	14 - 5	18 - 10	15 - 6	14 - 6
12 - 7	14 - 10	19 - 7	18 - 11	9 - 4	16 - 10	20 - 9	11 - 6	20 - 10	13 - 10
7 - 3	17 - 10	13 - 7	16 - 5	15 - 5	15 - 12	10 - 5	17 - 6	16 - 8	20 - 11
16 - 9	21 - 9	20 - 12	9 - 5	22 - 12	12 - 4	8 - 4	13 - 8	15 - 4	19 - 9
14 - 3	13 - 9	19 - 8	16 - 6	21 - 11	9 - 6	11 - 8	10 - 4	17 - 7	12 - 8
12 - 5	9 - 3	19 - 11	15 - 7	18 - 9	10 - 3	23 - 12	22 - 11	18 - 7	16 - 12
13 - 6	13 - 3	16 - 4	21 - 12	22 - 10	19 - 12	12 - 6	21 - 10	11 - 7	18 - 8
17 - 12	24 - 12	16 - 7	15 - 3	14 - 11	12 - 3	18 - 6	16 - 11	10 - 7	23 - 11
17 - 5	6 - 3	12 - 9	18 - 12	14 - 4	13 - 4	15 - 8	11 - 4	11 - 3	17 - 11

Name _____   Date _____

16 − 10	9 − 3	18 − 10	11 − 6	9 − 5	10 − 3	10 − 7	11 − 8	10 − 6	17 − 8
16 − 11	10 − 4	23 − 12	13 − 10	15 − 10	13 − 3	14 − 4	15 − 4	15 − 3	14 − 5
9 − 4	13 − 4	16 − 7	15 − 7	24 − 12	15 − 8	17 − 10	17 − 5	22 − 11	13 − 8
8 − 3	20 − 8	7 − 3	14 − 11	20 − 12	18 − 11	11 − 5	13 − 9	17 − 7	14 − 6
19 − 11	10 − 5	11 − 3	8 − 5	12 − 7	17 − 6	12 − 8	17 − 12	18 − 6	21 − 11
14 − 10	20 − 11	7 − 4	13 − 5	15 − 11	13 − 6	21 − 9	12 − 6	17 − 11	14 − 8
21 − 12	9 − 6	14 − 7	15 − 9	16 − 12	19 − 8	16 − 4	8 − 4	19 − 7	16 − 5
12 − 9	18 − 7	11 − 4	19 − 10	22 − 12	12 − 5	21 − 10	20 − 9	15 − 6	12 − 4
13 − 7	6 − 3	16 − 8	18 − 9	18 − 12	22 − 10	20 − 10	11 − 7	14 − 3	23 − 11
17 − 9	15 − 12	14 − 9	12 − 3	16 − 9	18 − 8	15 − 5	19 − 12	19 − 9	16 − 6

15 - 7	14 - 11	11 - 5	13 - 3	19 - 7	14 - 6	8 - 4	21 - 11	12 - 8	14 - 7
20 - 9	15 - 11	18 - 10	11 - 7	15 - 12	10 - 4	12 - 4	18 - 11	20 - 10	12 - 5
9 - 3	23 - 11	11 - 3	14 - 5	22 - 11	16 - 12	17 - 6	20 - 8	13 - 6	20 - 12
13 - 5	12 - 6	14 - 9	15 - 10	8 - 5	18 - 9	15 - 3	18 - 6	17 - 11	19 - 11
21 - 12	21 - 9	13 - 9	16 - 9	22 - 12	16 - 5	13 - 8	8 - 3	12 - 9	17 - 7
19 - 12	13 - 4	19 - 10	14 - 3	17 - 8	23 - 12	15 - 6	6 - 3	9 - 5	17 - 5
11 - 6	14 - 10	18 - 7	12 - 7	16 - 7	14 - 4	10 - 3	19 - 8	10 - 5	7 - 3
13 - 7	18 - 12	21 - 10	13 - 10	16 - 4	15 - 8	24 - 12	11 - 8	10 - 7	16 - 10
12 - 3	17 - 12	15 - 5	9 - 6	15 - 9	19 - 9	16 - 11	16 - 6	17 - 9	22 - 10
7 - 4	17 - 10	16 - 8	18 - 8	11 - 4	10 - 6	14 - 8	15 - 4	9 - 4	20 - 11

13 - 10	14 - 11	13 - 8	20 - 11	10 - 3	14 - 4	9 - 3	11 - 3	22 - 10	13 - 6
13 - 5	17 - 12	16 - 6	13 - 9	18 - 9	10 - 4	12 - 6	8 - 5	20 - 9	14 - 8
18 - 12	19 - 11	16 - 5	14 - 5	9 - 5	18 - 11	16 - 4	11 - 5	23 - 12	14 - 6
21 - 12	12 - 7	21 - 9	13 - 3	16 - 8	17 - 5	17 - 11	15 - 8	18 - 6	10 - 5
19 - 7	10 - 7	23 - 11	16 - 11	14 - 7	15 - 5	15 - 9	20 - 12	9 - 6	21 - 10
8 - 4	9 - 4	18 - 10	18 - 8	21 - 11	11 - 7	14 - 9	17 - 9	12 - 8	19 - 8
15 - 3	11 - 8	15 - 11	22 - 11	13 - 4	13 - 7	16 - 9	17 - 10	7 - 3	11 - 6
12 - 5	18 - 7	14 - 10	8 - 3	24 - 12	15 - 7	17 - 6	17 - 8	15 - 4	7 - 4
12 - 4	16 - 7	15 - 12	10 - 6	19 - 10	20 - 8	12 - 3	19 - 9	22 - 12	20 - 10
17 - 7	12 - 9	16 - 10	14 - 3	15 - 10	15 - 6	16 - 12	11 - 4	6 - 3	19 - 12

16 − 7	8 − 5	16 − 5	17 − 10	17 − 8	21 − 11	10 − 3	14 − 10	18 − 7	11 − 3
12 − 4	20 − 10	16 − 10	17 − 6	12 − 5	9 − 5	15 − 11	9 − 3	6 − 3	9 − 6
12 − 9	21 − 12	14 − 9	17 − 5	23 − 12	20 − 8	14 − 6	12 − 7	16 − 11	15 − 9
10 − 5	17 − 9	11 − 7	10 − 4	18 − 8	19 − 11	14 − 3	11 − 4	19 − 8	15 − 3
13 − 8	7 − 3	14 − 11	17 − 11	15 − 6	21 − 9	18 − 10	18 − 11	7 − 4	17 − 7
12 − 3	13 − 4	19 − 7	16 − 6	15 − 5	11 − 6	22 − 10	10 − 7	19 − 10	12 − 6
14 − 4	8 − 4	11 − 5	20 − 11	16 − 8	21 − 10	20 − 12	14 − 5	18 − 12	22 − 12
19 − 9	15 − 4	13 − 6	15 − 10	15 − 12	14 − 7	9 − 4	22 − 11	18 − 6	13 − 10
10 − 6	16 − 12	8 − 3	17 − 12	15 − 8	16 − 4	19 − 12	13 − 7	13 − 5	12 − 8
13 − 3	13 − 9	20 − 9	23 − 11	18 − 9	11 − 8	16 − 9	14 − 8	24 − 12	15 − 7

Name _____ Date _____

17 - 12	16 - 9	14 - 7	22 - 10	22 - 12	8 - 4	12 - 3	17 - 8	15 - 8	16 - 12
17 - 6	7 - 4	15 - 10	9 - 3	13 - 10	14 - 9	17 - 9	18 - 11	20 - 8	24 - 12
12 - 6	15 - 7	19 - 11	20 - 12	17 - 5	21 - 12	15 - 4	12 - 8	18 - 12	15 - 3
13 - 9	19 - 7	20 - 11	12 - 7	19 - 9	13 - 6	23 - 12	11 - 5	16 - 6	7 - 3
20 - 9	17 - 11	16 - 4	13 - 3	21 - 11	16 - 11	10 - 7	9 - 4	11 - 3	19 - 12
6 - 3	12 - 9	19 - 10	11 - 4	14 - 8	16 - 10	12 - 5	17 - 7	11 - 7	16 - 5
11 - 6	11 - 8	13 - 5	19 - 8	14 - 3	18 - 10	14 - 5	22 - 11	8 - 5	23 - 11
20 - 10	13 - 7	18 - 8	21 - 9	12 - 4	18 - 9	15 - 9	16 - 8	8 - 3	10 - 4
18 - 6	14 - 11	13 - 4	14 - 6	16 - 7	15 - 6	10 - 6	18 - 7	21 - 10	13 - 8
15 - 12	10 - 5	9 - 6	14 - 4	10 - 3	15 - 5	9 - 5	14 - 10	17 - 10	15 - 11

14 - 4	11 - 7	16 - 9	15 - 8	11 - 8	19 - 10	10 - 7	18 - 8	18 - 10	11 - 6
15 - 11	20 - 12	15 - 5	15 - 4	20 - 8	16 - 7	12 - 7	22 - 11	15 - 7	21 - 11
14 - 7	21 - 12	20 - 11	8 - 4	19 - 11	19 - 12	18 - 7	12 - 8	14 - 11	17 - 10
13 - 7	12 - 3	12 - 9	17 - 8	12 - 4	12 - 5	16 - 5	22 - 12	13 - 6	8 - 3
16 - 6	7 - 4	18 - 12	15 - 6	9 - 4	21 - 9	13 - 8	14 - 8	10 - 6	22 - 10
19 - 8	18 - 11	10 - 4	19 - 7	9 - 5	20 - 10	14 - 5	16 - 12	15 - 9	17 - 5
10 - 3	21 - 10	23 - 12	18 - 9	12 - 6	17 - 11	17 - 6	13 - 3	13 - 10	11 - 4
23 - 11	14 - 6	17 - 7	7 - 3	17 - 12	15 - 3	20 - 9	16 - 11	8 - 5	16 - 8
6 - 3	16 - 4	24 - 12	18 - 6	19 - 9	15 - 10	13 - 9	11 - 3	14 - 9	14 - 3
16 - 10	15 - 12	13 - 4	14 - 10	9 - 3	13 - 5	10 - 5	11 - 5	17 - 9	9 - 6

Name _____   Date _____

14	18	18	21	15	17	23	24	12	19
- 5	- 11	- 8	- 10	- 5	- 7	- 11	- 12	- 5	- 8

6	14	15	18	19	16	14	16	10	7
- 3	- 7	- 8	- 12	- 9	- 7	- 4	- 10	- 5	- 4

11	15	13	13	11	20	8	14	12	11
- 3	- 12	- 3	- 5	- 4	- 8	- 4	- 8	- 3	- 5

12	15	22	19	13	7	17	11	8	21
- 6	- 3	- 11	- 10	- 4	- 3	- 10	- 8	- 5	- 11

16	10	16	9	20	14	20	15	12	19
- 12	- 3	- 11	- 5	- 11	- 9	- 9	- 11	- 9	- 12

16	13	10	15	12	9	16	16	17	13
- 4	- 6	- 4	- 4	- 8	- 3	- 8	- 5	- 12	- 7

18	13	19	21	16	14	14	17	22	17
- 9	- 8	- 7	- 9	- 6	- 6	- 10	- 11	- 12	- 6

15	12	16	17	22	19	15	20	11	18
- 9	- 4	- 9	- 9	- 10	- 11	- 10	- 12	- 6	- 7

15	9	10	17	15	17	11	8	10	12
- 6	- 6	- 6	- 5	- 7	- 8	- 7	- 3	- 7	- 7

23	13	9	14	18	20	14	21	13	18
- 12	- 10	- 4	- 11	- 10	- 10	- 3	- 12	- 9	- 6

14 − 6	17 −11	21 −12	13 − 3	12 − 6	15 − 3	16 −12	18 − 7	18 − 9	15 −11
14 − 5	14 − 9	9 − 4	22 −10	18 −12	7 − 3	8 − 3	11 − 5	23 −12	17 − 7
14 − 7	12 − 7	20 −11	9 − 3	13 − 6	12 − 4	19 −10	13 − 5	14 − 3	17 − 6
10 − 6	15 − 5	21 −11	15 −12	13 − 8	20 −10	19 − 7	12 − 9	12 − 5	19 − 8
17 − 5	15 − 6	15 − 7	17 −12	17 − 8	14 −11	20 − 8	12 − 3	14 −10	13 −10
16 − 9	7 − 4	14 − 4	16 −11	12 − 8	11 − 6	24 −12	14 − 8	20 −12	13 − 4
19 − 9	22 −11	17 − 9	19 −12	16 − 4	8 − 5	11 − 3	13 − 7	6 − 3	9 − 6
10 − 5	10 − 7	13 − 9	21 − 9	10 − 4	21 −10	23 −11	19 −11	15 − 4	11 − 7
11 − 4	11 − 8	9 − 5	22 −12	18 − 6	8 − 4	20 − 9	18 −11	16 − 5	15 − 8
18 − 8	17 −10	10 − 3	18 −10	16 − 6	16 −10	16 − 8	16 − 7	15 − 9	15 −10

Name _____   Date _____

23 - 12	18 - 10	14 - 3	15 - 12	17 - 7	13 - 3	17 - 12	13 - 7	10 - 5	11 - 5
14 - 10	12 - 8	15 - 6	22 - 11	21 - 10	20 - 8	18 - 9	15 - 8	21 - 11	10 - 6
13 - 4	15 - 5	12 - 6	10 - 4	8 - 5	7 - 4	18 - 12	20 - 12	21 - 12	17 - 10
15 - 3	13 - 5	14 - 11	15 - 10	12 - 5	17 - 11	12 - 3	9 - 3	13 - 10	13 - 6
9 - 6	15 - 4	18 - 6	14 - 7	19 - 10	11 - 3	20 - 11	12 - 4	14 - 9	19 - 11
9 - 5	17 - 9	19 - 8	19 - 7	23 - 11	16 - 6	18 - 11	10 - 3	16 - 7	18 - 8
15 - 9	11 - 4	10 - 7	24 - 12	14 - 4	18 - 7	11 - 6	13 - 8	15 - 7	6 - 3
16 - 10	12 - 7	12 - 9	22 - 10	14 - 5	16 - 8	19 - 9	15 - 11	16 - 11	17 - 8
14 - 8	16 - 5	14 - 6	19 - 12	21 - 9	16 - 12	16 - 4	8 - 4	9 - 4	20 - 9
8 - 3	11 - 8	7 - 3	16 - 9	17 - 5	17 - 6	20 - 10	22 - 12	13 - 9	11 - 7

Name _____   Date _____

13	20	8	22	16	9	12	12	10	13
- 3	- 12	- 4	- 10	- 5	- 4	- 4	- 9	- 3	- 4

19	17	11	21	15	7	14	17	14	15
- 10	- 8	- 7	- 11	- 9	- 4	- 9	- 12	- 7	- 3

9	17	10	20	13	13	16	16	14	11
- 3	- 11	- 4	- 10	- 10	- 7	- 11	- 10	- 5	- 5

10	16	17	24	8	14	11	15	17	15
- 7	- 8	- 5	- 12	- 5	- 6	- 4	- 10	- 9	- 12

15	12	13	20	21	18	19	18	13	11
- 6	- 7	- 5	- 11	- 12	- 10	- 12	- 9	- 9	- 3

21	20	22	18	16	14	13	9	11	6
- 9	- 9	- 11	- 12	- 7	- 3	- 8	- 5	- 6	- 3

12	16	10	13	23	12	18	15	23	14
- 6	- 9	- 6	- 6	- 11	- 5	- 11	- 7	- 12	- 4

14	16	15	18	12	19	21	8	20	14
- 8	- 12	- 8	- 6	- 3	- 8	- 10	- 3	- 8	- 11

19	15	7	16	19	15	22	17	18	15
- 7	- 4	- 3	- 6	- 11	- 5	- 12	- 6	- 8	- 11

17	16	9	12	10	17	18	14	11	19
- 10	- 4	- 6	- 8	- 5	- 7	- 7	- 10	- 8	- 9

Name _____   Date _____

8 − 5	12 − 9	8 − 3	21 − 9	17 − 8	15 − 9	20 − 10	16 − 7	12 − 4	8 − 4
13 − 9	14 − 10	22 − 10	9 − 5	13 − 8	17 − 9	16 − 6	14 − 8	7 − 3	15 − 7
13 − 3	15 − 3	13 − 6	11 − 6	12 − 5	14 − 9	6 − 3	19 − 9	22 − 12	16 − 9
17 − 7	16 − 12	15 − 11	11 − 7	21 − 10	14 − 5	16 − 8	10 − 7	18 − 10	14 − 7
23 − 12	16 − 11	17 − 11	11 − 5	13 − 5	10 − 4	20 − 12	10 − 6	11 − 3	16 − 10
19 − 12	14 − 6	9 − 6	15 − 10	19 − 11	12 − 3	20 − 8	18 − 8	19 − 8	21 − 12
18 − 9	22 − 11	21 − 11	17 − 6	10 − 5	18 − 11	18 − 6	16 − 4	18 − 12	14 − 4
12 − 7	12 − 6	19 − 7	15 − 4	7 − 4	17 − 5	17 − 10	15 − 12	13 − 10	9 − 3
24 − 12	16 − 5	10 − 3	11 − 8	12 − 8	14 − 3	14 − 11	20 − 9	15 − 5	19 − 10
13 − 7	11 − 4	20 − 11	18 − 7	17 − 12	15 − 6	23 − 11	15 − 8	9 − 4	13 − 4

Name _____   Date _____

12 - 6	11 - 3	10 - 4	13 - 5	17 - 6	14 - 8	15 - 4	9 - 5	19 - 11	18 - 7
14 - 10	15 - 10	12 - 4	17 - 7	8 - 3	15 - 12	10 - 7	17 - 8	15 - 6	14 - 3
11 - 6	11 - 8	14 - 7	21 - 11	7 - 3	14 - 9	16 - 6	13 - 3	19 - 10	10 - 3
13 - 10	19 - 12	21 - 9	13 - 4	15 - 3	17 - 12	16 - 5	18 - 12	12 - 5	16 - 9
23 - 12	9 - 3	17 - 9	14 - 4	16 - 11	18 - 8	18 - 10	9 - 4	15 - 11	15 - 9
18 - 11	11 - 4	18 - 6	17 - 11	16 - 12	20 - 12	10 - 6	13 - 6	19 - 8	16 - 4
18 - 9	8 - 5	8 - 4	20 - 10	15 - 7	11 - 5	10 - 5	20 - 9	22 - 10	11 - 7
7 - 4	15 - 5	12 - 7	9 - 6	14 - 6	15 - 8	21 - 12	21 - 10	19 - 7	13 - 8
23 - 11	17 - 10	16 - 8	12 - 9	6 - 3	16 - 10	20 - 11	17 - 5	24 - 12	14 - 5
20 - 8	13 - 7	16 - 7	14 - 11	22 - 11	19 - 9	13 - 9	12 - 3	22 - 12	12 - 8

12	12	20	10	17	9	21	15	7	11
- 8	- 9	-12	- 5	- 6	- 4	-12	-10	- 3	- 5

13	14	20	17	15	12	18	18	10	19
- 9	-10	-11	- 9	- 9	- 7	- 6	-11	- 3	-11

13	17	16	12	21	21	13	12	10	13
- 4	-12	-10	- 3	-11	-10	- 5	- 4	- 7	- 3

11	20	15	17	10	6	11	17	10	20
- 4	-10	-11	- 8	- 6	- 3	- 7	-11	- 4	- 8

23	15	15	18	16	17	13	15	19	21
-12	-12	- 4	- 8	- 8	- 7	- 8	- 3	-12	- 9

8	23	11	22	16	12	16	16	16	19
- 3	-11	- 6	-11	-11	- 5	-12	- 9	- 7	- 7

14	7	18	14	16	13	15	9	14	14
-11	- 4	-12	- 7	- 6	-10	- 5	- 3	- 3	- 8

15	17	8	18	13	19	24	12	18	16
- 7	-10	- 5	- 9	- 7	- 9	-12	- 6	- 7	- 4

15	8	14	15	9	16	19	11	19	14
- 8	- 4	- 6	- 6	- 5	- 5	- 8	- 3	-10	- 5

17	14	9	20	18	14	22	22	13	11
- 5	- 9	- 6	- 9	-10	- 4	-10	-12	- 6	- 8

11 - 4	18 - 10	16 - 6	11 - 5	14 - 11	12 - 9	14 - 6	15 - 10	12 - 7	20 - 10
14 - 4	11 - 3	18 - 9	13 - 6	22 - 11	14 - 10	19 - 8	9 - 4	23 - 12	16 - 9
21 - 10	22 - 10	20 - 12	21 - 11	8 - 5	13 - 4	9 - 5	7 - 3	10 - 3	14 - 7
17 - 11	21 - 12	21 - 9	16 - 8	24 - 12	15 - 12	11 - 8	15 - 11	11 - 6	12 - 3
10 - 6	14 - 3	19 - 7	8 - 4	19 - 9	13 - 3	13 - 10	15 - 7	16 - 12	15 - 6
20 - 9	10 - 7	18 - 12	13 - 5	17 - 8	23 - 11	16 - 5	17 - 12	17 - 9	16 - 10
14 - 8	17 - 6	15 - 3	6 - 3	19 - 12	13 - 7	18 - 8	19 - 11	12 - 6	18 - 11
13 - 8	16 - 7	15 - 8	15 - 9	19 - 10	15 - 5	17 - 10	14 - 9	15 - 4	17 - 7
13 - 9	9 - 3	17 - 5	16 - 11	22 - 12	14 - 5	20 - 8	10 - 4	8 - 3	16 - 4
11 - 7	12 - 5	12 - 8	9 - 6	18 - 7	10 - 5	7 - 4	20 - 11	12 - 4	18 - 6

Name _____   Date _____

16 - 12	8 - 4	11 - 7	14 - 6	10 - 6	13 - 10	13 - 7	13 - 8	12 - 5	11 - 6
16 - 7	20 - 12	13 - 5	16 - 5	18 - 6	17 - 8	24 - 12	14 - 10	13 - 6	11 - 5
13 - 9	15 - 9	16 - 4	11 - 8	17 - 12	21 - 11	10 - 4	6 - 3	19 - 10	14 - 11
21 - 10	19 - 7	15 - 10	18 - 11	19 - 11	19 - 9	16 - 8	13 - 3	12 - 9	9 - 4
7 - 4	15 - 4	17 - 6	12 - 3	9 - 6	11 - 3	20 - 9	22 - 12	16 - 9	17 - 7
19 - 8	22 - 11	18 - 10	10 - 5	12 - 6	15 - 6	14 - 8	16 - 10	12 - 7	12 - 8
17 - 10	22 - 10	10 - 3	20 - 11	12 - 4	9 - 3	15 - 5	16 - 6	23 - 12	18 - 8
8 - 5	14 - 5	15 - 3	18 - 7	14 - 3	11 - 4	21 - 9	15 - 8	20 - 10	8 - 3
15 - 11	18 - 9	21 - 12	7 - 3	18 - 12	9 - 5	15 - 12	16 - 11	17 - 9	19 - 12
10 - 7	17 - 5	14 - 7	13 - 4	20 - 8	14 - 4	23 - 11	17 - 11	14 - 9	15 - 7

Name _____ Date _____

12 − 7	14 − 8	8 − 4	12 − 5	16 − 9	10 − 3	9 − 4	20 − 10	8 − 5	22 − 12
15 − 3	12 − 3	18 − 11	19 − 12	17 − 11	17 − 7	20 − 12	23 − 11	13 − 6	8 − 3
21 − 11	17 − 12	21 − 9	15 − 9	7 − 3	9 − 6	17 − 5	14 − 7	15 − 12	12 − 8
12 − 9	16 − 11	15 − 6	21 − 12	16 − 8	17 − 8	14 − 3	20 − 9	14 − 6	20 − 8
13 − 10	11 − 7	10 − 6	18 − 10	15 − 10	10 − 5	16 − 6	17 − 9	11 − 5	18 − 6
19 − 9	16 − 5	18 − 7	19 − 7	16 − 4	14 − 4	13 − 9	14 − 11	9 − 3	16 − 7
13 − 3	17 − 10	13 − 4	19 − 8	14 − 5	6 − 3	20 − 11	18 − 12	15 − 7	16 − 10
19 − 11	19 − 10	11 − 6	12 − 6	7 − 4	18 − 9	18 − 8	11 − 8	22 − 10	15 − 4
15 − 8	15 − 11	11 − 3	22 − 11	14 − 9	21 − 10	9 − 5	13 − 7	11 − 4	23 − 12
15 − 5	24 − 12	13 − 8	10 − 7	10 − 4	13 − 5	12 − 4	17 − 6	14 − 10	16 − 12

20 − 12	6 − 3	16 − 12	14 − 8	19 − 10	16 − 11	17 − 5	10 − 7	13 − 7	12 − 8
16 − 6	13 − 5	18 − 6	13 − 4	18 − 9	22 − 12	16 − 4	10 − 4	14 − 6	15 − 11
7 − 4	14 − 7	16 − 5	20 − 9	22 − 10	12 − 9	11 − 3	23 − 11	17 − 12	8 − 5
12 − 4	22 − 11	19 − 12	7 − 3	24 − 12	13 − 6	19 − 9	14 − 10	11 − 8	12 − 7
16 − 10	14 − 4	14 − 5	10 − 6	15 − 3	15 − 4	17 − 9	21 − 10	17 − 6	16 − 8
12 − 6	18 − 8	20 − 11	12 − 5	15 − 10	13 − 9	15 − 8	17 − 8	13 − 3	21 − 12
18 − 12	10 − 5	20 − 10	15 − 6	11 − 5	18 − 11	21 − 9	14 − 3	23 − 12	20 − 8
9 − 4	8 − 3	8 − 4	15 − 9	9 − 5	11 − 7	15 − 5	13 − 10	16 − 7	9 − 6
9 − 3	17 − 11	16 − 9	18 − 10	12 − 3	15 − 12	15 − 7	11 − 4	10 − 3	21 − 11
14 − 9	19 − 8	14 − 11	11 − 6	19 − 7	17 − 10	19 − 11	17 − 7	18 − 7	13 − 8

Name _____   Date _____

17 - 6	10 - 3	19 - 7	13 - 4	19 -12	6 - 3	16 - 7	22 -11	9 - 3	15 - 9
16 - 5	15 -10	16 - 4	17 - 9	16 -12	16 -10	10 - 6	15 -12	14 - 5	11 - 5
18 - 9	18 - 7	20 -10	21 - 9	11 - 4	24 -12	15 - 5	13 - 7	12 - 5	16 - 9
15 - 8	8 - 3	15 -11	9 - 6	17 - 8	12 - 3	7 - 4	9 - 4	18 - 8	21 -10
14 - 3	14 -11	7 - 3	20 - 8	23 -12	10 - 7	22 -12	12 - 7	20 -12	21 -11
18 -12	12 - 9	8 - 5	14 - 4	14 - 6	13 - 3	15 - 7	19 -11	21 -12	13 -10
20 -11	14 - 7	14 - 8	12 - 4	15 - 6	13 - 6	19 - 8	12 - 6	13 - 9	18 -10
16 - 8	17 -12	20 - 9	10 - 5	13 - 8	17 - 7	19 - 9	19 -10	16 -11	22 -10
17 -10	14 - 9	15 - 4	8 - 4	18 - 6	11 - 8	17 - 5	9 - 5	10 - 4	17 -11
11 - 3	23 -11	13 - 5	11 - 6	16 - 6	12 - 8	11 - 7	15 - 3	18 -11	14 -10

10 - 5	22 - 10	11 - 7	14 - 4	13 - 6	11 - 3	8 - 3	19 - 9	22 - 12	9 - 3
15 - 5	12 - 3	15 - 11	14 - 8	19 - 11	23 - 12	13 - 7	13 - 3	17 - 6	15 - 12
14 - 10	11 - 4	12 - 7	18 - 8	22 - 11	8 - 5	20 - 9	17 - 7	19 - 7	11 - 5
12 - 8	10 - 6	12 - 6	18 - 6	18 - 10	14 - 6	17 - 10	16 - 8	19 - 12	10 - 4
24 - 12	11 - 8	7 - 3	16 - 11	16 - 4	12 - 5	12 - 9	14 - 5	19 - 8	21 - 11
13 - 9	13 - 4	16 - 5	15 - 7	20 - 11	17 - 8	20 - 12	16 - 10	14 - 11	16 - 6
20 - 10	21 - 12	11 - 6	13 - 8	17 - 11	10 - 3	21 - 9	8 - 4	16 - 12	7 - 4
13 - 10	17 - 5	9 - 6	9 - 5	18 - 12	16 - 9	15 - 8	15 - 10	18 - 11	17 - 9
18 - 9	9 - 4	19 - 10	18 - 7	13 - 5	15 - 3	14 - 3	10 - 7	15 - 9	6 - 3
12 - 4	23 - 11	16 - 7	15 - 4	17 - 12	14 - 7	21 - 10	14 - 9	20 - 8	15 - 6

Name _____ Date _____

13 - 10	20 - 12	23 - 11	14 - 7	9 - 5	11 - 7	13 - 3	13 - 5	22 - 12	16 - 7
9 - 4	14 - 9	8 - 3	18 - 6	16 - 5	20 - 11	21 - 10	19 - 7	11 - 5	16 - 10
19 - 12	18 - 9	7 - 4	17 - 6	10 - 7	14 - 3	14 - 6	11 - 8	14 - 8	19 - 11
16 - 11	15 - 12	13 - 8	12 - 5	10 - 3	13 - 7	15 - 4	14 - 11	17 - 5	13 - 9
24 - 12	13 - 6	21 - 12	15 - 8	12 - 4	12 - 9	18 - 7	8 - 4	17 - 10	16 - 6
17 - 7	15 - 10	15 - 6	14 - 5	17 - 9	14 - 4	20 - 10	20 - 9	17 - 12	15 - 9
21 - 11	11 - 3	16 - 9	18 - 8	15 - 3	19 - 8	13 - 4	19 - 9	10 - 6	9 - 3
8 - 5	12 - 3	18 - 12	22 - 10	21 - 9	9 - 6	11 - 6	16 - 4	20 - 8	15 - 7
12 - 7	15 - 11	15 - 5	16 - 12	12 - 6	18 - 11	10 - 5	18 - 10	23 - 12	17 - 11
6 - 3	7 - 3	11 - 4	14 - 10	12 - 8	22 - 11	16 - 8	19 - 10	10 - 4	17 - 8

15 - 5	18 - 9	10 - 3	16 -11	14 - 6	7 - 3	12 - 5	19 -10	15 - 4	11 - 4
16 -12	19 - 8	17 -11	16 - 6	21 -12	14 - 3	13 - 4	17 - 7	16 -10	14 -10
8 - 5	20 -11	12 - 4	20 -12	15 - 8	15 -10	18 -11	24 -12	9 - 5	11 - 3
18 -12	10 - 4	15 - 3	14 - 9	17 -12	21 - 9	11 - 7	13 - 6	10 - 6	15 - 7
16 - 5	12 - 6	19 -12	20 - 9	22 -11	14 -11	23 -12	8 - 3	11 - 5	19 - 9
8 - 4	14 - 4	20 -10	13 -10	12 - 8	18 - 8	21 -10	17 - 5	9 - 3	13 - 8
17 -10	15 -11	18 -10	15 - 6	11 - 6	13 - 3	6 - 3	13 - 9	22 -12	13 - 5
15 - 9	16 - 7	20 - 8	15 -12	14 - 8	16 - 9	21 -11	9 - 4	13 - 7	18 - 6
10 - 7	22 -10	16 - 8	14 - 7	12 - 9	12 - 3	19 -11	19 - 7	9 - 6	14 - 5
23 -11	12 - 7	7 - 4	11 - 8	16 - 4	17 - 6	18 - 7	10 - 5	17 - 9	17 - 8

Name _____   Date _____

8 - 4	14 - 10	18 - 10	21 - 11	19 - 12	11 - 4	14 - 3	16 - 12	16 - 4	16 - 7
14 - 8	17 - 10	14 - 7	16 - 8	20 - 9	16 - 10	7 - 3	19 - 10	18 - 8	10 - 4
10 - 3	15 - 3	13 - 9	17 - 9	11 - 6	14 - 11	15 - 8	10 - 7	23 - 11	13 - 5
18 - 7	20 - 8	18 - 9	16 - 9	23 - 12	6 - 3	19 - 7	13 - 3	20 - 10	11 - 8
10 - 5	15 - 11	22 - 10	13 - 7	22 - 11	17 - 12	17 - 8	15 - 7	16 - 5	12 - 4
15 - 10	9 - 4	12 - 7	15 - 5	21 - 12	15 - 6	19 - 9	15 - 4	22 - 12	17 - 11
21 - 9	14 - 4	14 - 5	12 - 5	20 - 11	8 - 3	17 - 7	12 - 6	8 - 5	12 - 8
9 - 6	15 - 12	11 - 7	9 - 5	13 - 10	13 - 8	13 - 4	10 - 6	19 - 11	15 - 9
12 - 9	17 - 6	7 - 4	16 - 6	9 - 3	18 - 11	18 - 6	24 - 12	18 - 12	12 - 3
11 - 3	14 - 6	20 - 12	13 - 6	21 - 10	11 - 5	19 - 8	17 - 5	16 - 11	14 - 9

Name _____ Date _____

12 × 8	12 × 0	7 × 9	9 × 9	11 × 3	4 × 2	12 × 1	12 × 12	9 × 12	2 × 0
2 × 8	0 × 2	11 × 12	6 × 5	3 × 12	0 × 4	0 × 8	3 × 5	8 × 11	2 × 3
6 × 9	10 × 2	1 × 4	5 × 11	3 × 9	3 × 1	7 × 8	9 × 1	3 × 11	0 × 6
7 × 4	12 × 3	6 × 2	8 × 8	4 × 0	12 × 7	8 × 1	0 × 1	11 × 8	7 × 12
5 × 1	3 × 6	4 × 6	7 × 10	0 × 11	6 × 4	5 × 4	6 × 6	5 × 12	10 × 6
10 × 12	9 × 11	6 × 7	1 × 2	6 × 3	2 × 6	10 × 4	4 × 7	2 × 7	8 × 9
5 × 10	10 × 8	5 × 9	4 × 9	3 × 3	11 × 11	1 × 6	11 × 2	10 × 1	3 × 2
9 × 4	5 × 5	4 × 12	10 × 7	10 × 3	0 × 10	9 × 8	12 × 4	6 × 0	7 × 6
9 × 5	7 × 2	8 × 7	1 × 7	2 × 4	2 × 11	0 × 7	2 × 2	7 × 7	11 × 7
7 × 1	5 × 8	6 × 12	2 × 1	1 × 3	5 × 6	0 × 5	11 × 4	6 × 10	8 × 6

Name _____ Date _____

9 × 5	1 × 7	9 × 0	6 × 8	6 × 4	10 × 0	8 × 4	12 × 7	10 × 2	12 × 4
12 × 8	5 × 8	10 × 6	5 × 9	5 × 0	0 × 2	4 × 0	3 × 2	9 × 7	7 × 5
8 × 8	2 × 7	2 × 5	1 × 1	2 × 6	12 × 1	1 × 9	1 × 5	8 × 10	3 × 11
7 × 2	8 × 3	0 × 8	1 × 3	3 × 12	8 × 12	9 × 1	2 × 11	0 × 5	10 × 5
3 × 4	7 × 1	5 × 7	5 × 11	6 × 7	11 × 8	7 × 12	8 × 0	10 × 10	11 × 5
7 × 9	3 × 8	1 × 0	10 × 11	9 × 3	0 × 11	5 × 6	5 × 5	1 × 2	12 × 3
0 × 6	9 × 12	11 × 0	9 × 10	3 × 1	4 × 8	5 × 2	10 × 4	2 × 10	11 × 4
7 × 7	5 × 4	7 × 4	2 × 9	12 × 5	1 × 10	5 × 12	8 × 9	4 × 2	4 × 7
12 × 0	2 × 2	2 × 8	0 × 9	6 × 3	7 × 0	0 × 3	11 × 9	9 × 6	11 × 7
11 × 3	4 × 5	8 × 1	12 × 6	4 × 3	0 × 10	10 × 3	8 × 7	11 × 12	10 × 12

Name _____   Date _____

4 × 4	1 × 8	10 × 6	5 × 0	7 × 4	7 × 10	9 × 5	12 × 10	3 × 9	10 × 4
7 × 3	11 × 0	10 × 3	2 × 4	6 × 9	6 × 2	10 × 0	0 × 7	3 × 10	5 × 2
9 × 7	10 × 5	9 × 4	1 × 2	12 × 1	1 × 6	5 × 11	3 × 1	6 × 3	2 × 10
8 × 6	1 × 1	8 × 7	2 × 12	7 × 7	11 × 12	5 × 5	3 × 4	5 × 3	9 × 6
1 × 4	12 × 0	12 × 12	5 × 6	10 × 10	0 × 2	7 × 5	4 × 0	0 × 1	9 × 8
11 × 4	9 × 0	4 × 5	9 × 10	11 × 7	11 × 5	0 × 9	4 × 12	3 × 2	3 × 8
9 × 11	4 × 2	12 × 4	2 × 0	4 × 6	10 × 12	3 × 5	2 × 6	6 × 5	8 × 3
2 × 2	1 × 12	0 × 6	8 × 5	10 × 7	9 × 12	11 × 2	6 × 8	1 × 7	8 × 9
1 × 0	9 × 2	10 × 1	12 × 5	11 × 1	8 × 8	10 × 11	12 × 11	0 × 12	5 × 7
8 × 4	7 × 12	8 × 12	0 × 3	12 × 6	12 × 7	4 × 7	0 × 4	11 × 9	12 × 2

Name _____   Date _____

12 × 0	1 × 4	11 × 7	11 × 8	3 × 7	8 × 3	0 × 10	2 × 6	6 × 9	0 × 4
10 × 1	1 × 11	6 × 4	11 × 2	4 × 0	12 × 6	1 × 0	4 × 7	11 × 0	1 × 9
5 × 8	8 × 10	4 × 2	10 × 2	10 × 5	0 × 5	6 × 1	9 × 3	11 × 5	5 × 12
9 × 4	3 × 9	7 × 2	7 × 0	3 × 6	10 × 7	1 × 6	9 × 9	7 × 6	0 × 2
8 × 7	10 × 11	3 × 12	12 × 8	4 × 3	4 × 12	11 × 10	8 × 11	11 × 1	5 × 7
11 × 3	10 × 8	5 × 11	1 × 1	7 × 11	12 × 12	7 × 12	11 × 6	6 × 5	9 × 6
1 × 10	12 × 5	8 × 6	5 × 9	2 × 8	8 × 5	3 × 8	6 × 0	5 × 5	5 × 0
9 × 1	7 × 10	0 × 11	0 × 6	3 × 10	8 × 4	12 × 4	9 × 8	7 × 8	4 × 5
3 × 0	3 × 4	0 × 0	5 × 6	11 × 12	0 × 3	6 × 7	5 × 2	6 × 10	4 × 11
2 × 11	2 × 7	8 × 12	7 × 1	9 × 5	11 × 11	2 × 10	6 × 8	9 × 7	5 × 3

Name _____   Date _____

10 × 0	1 × 10	5 × 9	4 × 1	5 × 2	10 × 3	10 × 11	3 × 2	4 × 3	10 × 10
6 × 11	6 × 5	2 × 11	4 × 11	4 × 10	8 × 5	9 × 4	0 × 2	0 × 9	2 × 8
7 × 3	4 × 0	11 × 1	12 × 2	11 × 7	8 × 11	3 × 9	6 × 9	0 × 0	11 × 0
6 × 7	5 × 5	0 × 8	1 × 8	0 × 12	12 × 3	11 × 4	12 × 10	6 × 4	5 × 4
2 × 2	10 × 2	8 × 0	9 × 6	11 × 6	11 × 10	1 × 1	10 × 8	8 × 12	1 × 9
9 × 12	12 × 9	9 × 8	0 × 10	5 × 0	10 × 5	7 × 6	11 × 9	6 × 3	4 × 5
3 × 4	3 × 7	12 × 12	6 × 1	8 × 2	1 × 6	3 × 11	9 × 2	0 × 3	3 × 0
12 × 6	11 × 3	3 × 12	2 × 9	5 × 1	2 × 0	7 × 4	7 × 0	12 × 4	12 × 1
10 × 6	9 × 3	5 × 7	0 × 7	2 × 6	6 × 8	7 × 11	9 × 0	4 × 7	2 × 7
6 × 2	1 × 7	11 × 8	5 × 8	2 × 5	5 × 3	4 × 2	3 × 5	7 × 12	9 × 9

Name _____ Date _____

$\begin{array}{r}5\\ \times\ 7\\\hline\end{array}$	$\begin{array}{r}4\\ \times\ 0\\\hline\end{array}$	$\begin{array}{r}6\\ \times\ 1\\\hline\end{array}$	$\begin{array}{r}9\\ \times\ 3\\\hline\end{array}$	$\begin{array}{r}4\\ \times\ 1\\\hline\end{array}$	$\begin{array}{r}7\\ \times\ 1\\\hline\end{array}$	$\begin{array}{r}6\\ \times\ 9\\\hline\end{array}$	$\begin{array}{r}11\\ \times\ 0\\\hline\end{array}$	$\begin{array}{r}0\\ \times\ 3\\\hline\end{array}$	$\begin{array}{r}3\\ \times\ 1\\\hline\end{array}$
$\begin{array}{r}2\\ \times\ 8\\\hline\end{array}$	$\begin{array}{r}2\\ \times\ 11\\\hline\end{array}$	$\begin{array}{r}3\\ \times\ 4\\\hline\end{array}$	$\begin{array}{r}8\\ \times\ 3\\\hline\end{array}$	$\begin{array}{r}7\\ \times\ 2\\\hline\end{array}$	$\begin{array}{r}12\\ \times\ 6\\\hline\end{array}$	$\begin{array}{r}11\\ \times\ 1\\\hline\end{array}$	$\begin{array}{r}10\\ \times\ 8\\\hline\end{array}$	$\begin{array}{r}3\\ \times\ 0\\\hline\end{array}$	$\begin{array}{r}6\\ \times\ 12\\\hline\end{array}$
$\begin{array}{r}12\\ \times\ 3\\\hline\end{array}$	$\begin{array}{r}3\\ \times\ 11\\\hline\end{array}$	$\begin{array}{r}5\\ \times\ 0\\\hline\end{array}$	$\begin{array}{r}4\\ \times\ 4\\\hline\end{array}$	$\begin{array}{r}8\\ \times\ 8\\\hline\end{array}$	$\begin{array}{r}6\\ \times\ 3\\\hline\end{array}$	$\begin{array}{r}12\\ \times\ 11\\\hline\end{array}$	$\begin{array}{r}6\\ \times\ 11\\\hline\end{array}$	$\begin{array}{r}11\\ \times\ 2\\\hline\end{array}$	$\begin{array}{r}6\\ \times\ 2\\\hline\end{array}$
$\begin{array}{r}12\\ \times\ 2\\\hline\end{array}$	$\begin{array}{r}4\\ \times\ 2\\\hline\end{array}$	$\begin{array}{r}11\\ \times\ 6\\\hline\end{array}$	$\begin{array}{r}0\\ \times\ 10\\\hline\end{array}$	$\begin{array}{r}6\\ \times\ 6\\\hline\end{array}$	$\begin{array}{r}3\\ \times\ 7\\\hline\end{array}$	$\begin{array}{r}9\\ \times\ 5\\\hline\end{array}$	$\begin{array}{r}10\\ \times\ 3\\\hline\end{array}$	$\begin{array}{r}12\\ \times\ 7\\\hline\end{array}$	$\begin{array}{r}8\\ \times\ 5\\\hline\end{array}$
$\begin{array}{r}2\\ \times\ 2\\\hline\end{array}$	$\begin{array}{r}5\\ \times\ 11\\\hline\end{array}$	$\begin{array}{r}10\\ \times\ 1\\\hline\end{array}$	$\begin{array}{r}6\\ \times\ 10\\\hline\end{array}$	$\begin{array}{r}4\\ \times\ 8\\\hline\end{array}$	$\begin{array}{r}2\\ \times\ 12\\\hline\end{array}$	$\begin{array}{r}6\\ \times\ 7\\\hline\end{array}$	$\begin{array}{r}1\\ \times\ 10\\\hline\end{array}$	$\begin{array}{r}12\\ \times\ 1\\\hline\end{array}$	$\begin{array}{r}1\\ \times\ 5\\\hline\end{array}$
$\begin{array}{r}3\\ \times\ 6\\\hline\end{array}$	$\begin{array}{r}1\\ \times\ 12\\\hline\end{array}$	$\begin{array}{r}11\\ \times\ 11\\\hline\end{array}$	$\begin{array}{r}8\\ \times\ 1\\\hline\end{array}$	$\begin{array}{r}11\\ \times\ 7\\\hline\end{array}$	$\begin{array}{r}0\\ \times\ 1\\\hline\end{array}$	$\begin{array}{r}1\\ \times\ 3\\\hline\end{array}$	$\begin{array}{r}4\\ \times\ 3\\\hline\end{array}$	$\begin{array}{r}7\\ \times\ 6\\\hline\end{array}$	$\begin{array}{r}4\\ \times\ 12\\\hline\end{array}$
$\begin{array}{r}8\\ \times\ 10\\\hline\end{array}$	$\begin{array}{r}1\\ \times\ 11\\\hline\end{array}$	$\begin{array}{r}9\\ \times\ 8\\\hline\end{array}$	$\begin{array}{r}2\\ \times\ 3\\\hline\end{array}$	$\begin{array}{r}4\\ \times\ 9\\\hline\end{array}$	$\begin{array}{r}1\\ \times\ 1\\\hline\end{array}$	$\begin{array}{r}8\\ \times\ 11\\\hline\end{array}$	$\begin{array}{r}2\\ \times\ 7\\\hline\end{array}$	$\begin{array}{r}4\\ \times\ 7\\\hline\end{array}$	$\begin{array}{r}10\\ \times\ 5\\\hline\end{array}$
$\begin{array}{r}10\\ \times\ 9\\\hline\end{array}$	$\begin{array}{r}9\\ \times\ 4\\\hline\end{array}$	$\begin{array}{r}2\\ \times\ 5\\\hline\end{array}$	$\begin{array}{r}9\\ \times\ 7\\\hline\end{array}$	$\begin{array}{r}10\\ \times\ 7\\\hline\end{array}$	$\begin{array}{r}9\\ \times\ 2\\\hline\end{array}$	$\begin{array}{r}6\\ \times\ 8\\\hline\end{array}$	$\begin{array}{r}0\\ \times\ 4\\\hline\end{array}$	$\begin{array}{r}0\\ \times\ 11\\\hline\end{array}$	$\begin{array}{r}0\\ \times\ 9\\\hline\end{array}$
$\begin{array}{r}1\\ \times\ 8\\\hline\end{array}$	$\begin{array}{r}4\\ \times\ 6\\\hline\end{array}$	$\begin{array}{r}4\\ \times\ 11\\\hline\end{array}$	$\begin{array}{r}0\\ \times\ 0\\\hline\end{array}$	$\begin{array}{r}3\\ \times\ 3\\\hline\end{array}$	$\begin{array}{r}10\\ \times\ 0\\\hline\end{array}$	$\begin{array}{r}5\\ \times\ 2\\\hline\end{array}$	$\begin{array}{r}5\\ \times\ 8\\\hline\end{array}$	$\begin{array}{r}4\\ \times\ 5\\\hline\end{array}$	$\begin{array}{r}9\\ \times\ 6\\\hline\end{array}$
$\begin{array}{r}1\\ \times\ 2\\\hline\end{array}$	$\begin{array}{r}10\\ \times\ 10\\\hline\end{array}$	$\begin{array}{r}7\\ \times\ 7\\\hline\end{array}$	$\begin{array}{r}1\\ \times\ 9\\\hline\end{array}$	$\begin{array}{r}0\\ \times\ 5\\\hline\end{array}$	$\begin{array}{r}6\\ \times\ 4\\\hline\end{array}$	$\begin{array}{r}8\\ \times\ 0\\\hline\end{array}$	$\begin{array}{r}3\\ \times\ 8\\\hline\end{array}$	$\begin{array}{r}7\\ \times\ 8\\\hline\end{array}$	$\begin{array}{r}3\\ \times\ 5\\\hline\end{array}$

Name _____   Date _____

2 × 0	5 × 5	1 × 3	8 × 2	8 × 7	11 × 7	9 × 3	5 × 11	12 × 1	12 × 2
12 × 5	9 × 2	1 × 9	0 × 0	1 × 1	9 × 0	11 × 12	2 × 10	4 × 2	7 × 7
7 × 2	1 × 12	12 × 7	4 × 4	3 × 11	6 × 11	2 × 6	6 × 2	12 × 11	10 × 10
8 × 6	11 × 0	11 × 5	4 × 0	12 × 6	8 × 11	10 × 3	6 × 3	5 × 12	0 × 5
11 × 11	0 × 1	6 × 5	3 × 2	1 × 6	1 × 5	11 × 10	7 × 5	0 × 11	6 × 12
1 × 10	10 × 5	3 × 10	7 × 8	12 × 10	1 × 0	9 × 1	2 × 9	0 × 9	6 × 6
3 × 4	8 × 0	2 × 11	1 × 8	2 × 7	8 × 10	8 × 3	9 × 6	5 × 10	5 × 1
3 × 9	2 × 3	5 × 6	9 × 12	11 × 2	12 × 12	9 × 8	7 × 12	2 × 2	0 × 2
7 × 11	12 × 0	4 × 11	9 × 11	5 × 2	4 × 6	9 × 9	4 × 10	4 × 8	2 × 5
4 × 5	12 × 3	1 × 4	6 × 8	3 × 7	10 × 2	0 × 6	11 × 9	6 × 10	3 × 1

5 × 10	6 × 1	12 × 0	2 × 5	12 × 8	3 × 10	8 × 8	8 × 1	12 × 4	0 × 1
10 × 11	5 × 11	9 × 3	3 × 12	11 × 12	7 × 7	4 × 3	10 × 12	5 × 5	6 × 0
1 × 1	6 × 9	10 × 2	2 × 3	10 × 1	2 × 11	7 × 4	1 × 5	3 × 5	4 × 6
10 × 0	1 × 9	1 × 2	1 × 3	4 × 7	5 × 4	5 × 6	2 × 10	11 × 2	5 × 3
5 × 1	6 × 5	12 × 1	0 × 4	11 × 7	0 × 11	2 × 6	5 × 9	11 × 3	6 × 12
3 × 11	6 × 8	12 × 11	2 × 12	4 × 11	3 × 2	10 × 5	2 × 1	3 × 8	1 × 6
12 × 2	7 × 9	6 × 2	5 × 2	4 × 2	9 × 8	6 × 7	4 × 12	7 × 0	11 × 9
10 × 3	12 × 7	7 × 8	2 × 9	7 × 5	9 × 2	1 × 7	8 × 6	8 × 11	3 × 1
9 × 10	4 × 9	2 × 4	11 × 4	10 × 6	11 × 11	7 × 2	8 × 12	12 × 9	6 × 4
10 × 7	6 × 6	10 × 4	8 × 10	4 × 1	0 × 7	5 × 0	1 × 4	1 × 10	1 × 8

Name _____   Date _____

6 × 10	2 × 6	6 × 12	11 × 4	12 × 3	9 × 9	3 × 0	6 × 6	2 × 4	11 × 1
3 × 2	4 × 3	5 × 9	3 × 4	1 × 12	10 × 10	7 × 8	6 × 11	8 × 10	7 × 2
7 × 6	3 × 6	4 × 11	6 × 9	1 × 0	4 × 9	9 × 10	7 × 4	7 × 11	8 × 2
12 × 10	0 × 0	8 × 5	11 × 8	1 × 8	4 × 8	12 × 8	4 × 12	2 × 7	12 × 1
8 × 4	2 × 9	2 × 3	12 × 2	6 × 7	5 × 8	5 × 2	10 × 5	8 × 9	9 × 8
9 × 4	2 × 1	7 × 7	12 × 4	10 × 9	1 × 7	1 × 6	10 × 0	10 × 11	0 × 9
11 × 12	10 × 6	11 × 6	3 × 5	3 × 10	6 × 3	3 × 11	8 × 1	11 × 2	11 × 9
8 × 11	0 × 7	5 × 7	3 × 1	7 × 3	0 × 5	0 × 8	4 × 6	11 × 7	9 × 2
7 × 12	12 × 9	5 × 12	5 × 3	3 × 12	9 × 11	4 × 7	12 × 11	12 × 6	8 × 6
10 × 7	12 × 7	0 × 12	5 × 0	2 × 10	3 × 8	9 × 1	2 × 0	4 × 4	0 × 3

3 × 2	5 × 0	8 × 3	7 × 8	0 × 1	7 × 9	4 × 8	3 × 10	1 × 11	5 × 1
8 × 7	8 × 5	9 × 8	6 × 0	9 × 11	3 × 1	4 × 4	8 × 9	0 × 0	10 × 12
3 × 3	0 × 4	3 × 9	7 × 7	12 × 10	10 × 5	2 × 8	4 × 2	6 × 7	12 × 11
8 × 1	10 × 3	9 × 4	7 × 2	3 × 4	2 × 7	7 × 11	12 × 7	8 × 10	7 × 3
1 × 6	9 × 0	12 × 5	10 × 10	12 × 6	9 × 9	1 × 8	10 × 11	5 × 2	5 × 7
1 × 5	1 × 2	5 × 6	11 × 1	3 × 8	5 × 9	10 × 2	0 × 10	12 × 8	4 × 11
5 × 3	9 × 10	10 × 0	12 × 2	1 × 7	4 × 5	7 × 5	0 × 11	9 × 3	9 × 12
8 × 4	8 × 2	10 × 7	0 × 6	0 × 12	2 × 11	0 × 8	9 × 2	1 × 10	0 × 5
10 × 8	2 × 9	2 × 6	2 × 1	1 × 12	11 × 8	10 × 4	4 × 0	1 × 1	12 × 1
4 × 1	2 × 12	7 × 6	1 × 3	12 × 9	5 × 4	6 × 6	12 × 0	2 × 5	6 × 1

Name _____   Date _____

3 × 0	9 × 10	3 × 11	7 × 1	0 × 4	9 × 9	8 × 4	10 × 7	12 × 0	7 × 2
5 × 5	8 × 6	7 × 7	12 × 8	6 × 9	0 × 3	2 × 2	4 × 1	9 × 4	9 × 7
1 × 10	3 × 1	12 × 7	11 × 1	12 × 3	2 × 12	7 × 6	12 × 11	6 × 8	6 × 2
4 × 3	7 × 0	6 × 5	3 × 10	5 × 11	12 × 6	6 × 0	3 × 6	8 × 10	9 × 1
9 × 3	10 × 3	5 × 7	3 × 4	10 × 8	3 × 12	5 × 6	4 × 5	1 × 12	0 × 7
2 × 5	1 × 5	11 × 9	6 × 4	2 × 0	7 × 3	8 × 7	1 × 6	11 × 11	11 × 4
10 × 10	7 × 4	8 × 8	1 × 7	8 × 11	2 × 8	10 × 0	8 × 2	6 × 7	8 × 5
2 × 1	2 × 9	10 × 12	9 × 0	11 × 7	6 × 6	3 × 3	0 × 5	4 × 7	8 × 3
5 × 3	1 × 1	2 × 3	4 × 8	4 × 11	10 × 6	12 × 1	0 × 10	0 × 8	12 × 5
5 × 12	2 × 7	7 × 8	10 × 4	6 × 10	11 × 5	6 × 1	12 × 9	9 × 8	3 × 2

Name _____   Date _____

11 × 3	4 × 7	6 × 4	4 × 9	7 × 3	1 × 6	11 × 11	7 × 7	10 × 10	8 × 1
2 × 7	7 × 11	6 × 7	2 × 1	6 × 6	9 × 10	10 × 9	4 × 1	1 × 8	9 × 12
3 × 10	12 × 9	8 × 3	3 × 3	7 × 9	11 × 4	3 × 2	6 × 10	8 × 5	10 × 5
2 × 5	4 × 0	7 × 8	4 × 2	1 × 3	7 × 0	0 × 12	12 × 7	11 × 5	12 × 11
4 × 4	5 × 7	2 × 2	2 × 3	8 × 0	9 × 4	2 × 10	0 × 0	4 × 12	12 × 5
8 × 11	11 × 9	3 × 4	11 × 2	1 × 4	4 × 6	12 × 8	6 × 3	5 × 8	7 × 4
3 × 8	12 × 4	1 × 1	0 × 5	10 × 6	3 × 7	12 × 1	4 × 8	5 × 12	9 × 6
1 × 12	2 × 9	3 × 12	3 × 9	5 × 3	8 × 10	0 × 6	4 × 5	7 × 2	1 × 2
2 × 0	1 × 9	0 × 8	2 × 6	4 × 11	10 × 4	5 × 11	8 × 9	7 × 5	11 × 8
10 × 0	10 × 3	11 × 0	8 × 12	9 × 1	1 × 10	6 × 11	10 × 7	11 × 10	5 × 4

Name _____   Date _____

$\begin{array}{r}12\\ \times\ 0\end{array}$	$\begin{array}{r}5\\ \times\ 12\end{array}$	$\begin{array}{r}8\\ \times\ 0\end{array}$	$\begin{array}{r}2\\ \times\ 1\end{array}$	$\begin{array}{r}5\\ \times\ 0\end{array}$	$\begin{array}{r}12\\ \times\ 3\end{array}$	$\begin{array}{r}1\\ \times\ 7\end{array}$	$\begin{array}{r}12\\ \times\ 11\end{array}$	$\begin{array}{r}5\\ \times\ 3\end{array}$	$\begin{array}{r}3\\ \times\ 10\end{array}$
$\begin{array}{r}10\\ \times\ 7\end{array}$	$\begin{array}{r}12\\ \times\ 10\end{array}$	$\begin{array}{r}4\\ \times\ 7\end{array}$	$\begin{array}{r}7\\ \times\ 8\end{array}$	$\begin{array}{r}4\\ \times\ 8\end{array}$	$\begin{array}{r}4\\ \times\ 11\end{array}$	$\begin{array}{r}11\\ \times\ 2\end{array}$	$\begin{array}{r}10\\ \times\ 6\end{array}$	$\begin{array}{r}11\\ \times\ 10\end{array}$	$\begin{array}{r}6\\ \times\ 4\end{array}$
$\begin{array}{r}9\\ \times\ 9\end{array}$	$\begin{array}{r}0\\ \times\ 2\end{array}$	$\begin{array}{r}0\\ \times\ 6\end{array}$	$\begin{array}{r}8\\ \times\ 9\end{array}$	$\begin{array}{r}8\\ \times\ 3\end{array}$	$\begin{array}{r}7\\ \times\ 3\end{array}$	$\begin{array}{r}12\\ \times\ 2\end{array}$	$\begin{array}{r}5\\ \times\ 10\end{array}$	$\begin{array}{r}1\\ \times\ 6\end{array}$	$\begin{array}{r}5\\ \times\ 5\end{array}$
$\begin{array}{r}12\\ \times\ 5\end{array}$	$\begin{array}{r}12\\ \times\ 1\end{array}$	$\begin{array}{r}12\\ \times\ 12\end{array}$	$\begin{array}{r}2\\ \times\ 3\end{array}$	$\begin{array}{r}3\\ \times\ 2\end{array}$	$\begin{array}{r}7\\ \times\ 7\end{array}$	$\begin{array}{r}11\\ \times\ 8\end{array}$	$\begin{array}{r}11\\ \times\ 5\end{array}$	$\begin{array}{r}2\\ \times\ 12\end{array}$	$\begin{array}{r}9\\ \times\ 3\end{array}$
$\begin{array}{r}5\\ \times\ 6\end{array}$	$\begin{array}{r}0\\ \times\ 5\end{array}$	$\begin{array}{r}0\\ \times\ 3\end{array}$	$\begin{array}{r}4\\ \times\ 1\end{array}$	$\begin{array}{r}8\\ \times\ 5\end{array}$	$\begin{array}{r}3\\ \times\ 11\end{array}$	$\begin{array}{r}9\\ \times\ 2\end{array}$	$\begin{array}{r}10\\ \times\ 8\end{array}$	$\begin{array}{r}10\\ \times\ 4\end{array}$	$\begin{array}{r}0\\ \times\ 4\end{array}$
$\begin{array}{r}2\\ \times\ 9\end{array}$	$\begin{array}{r}2\\ \times\ 6\end{array}$	$\begin{array}{r}1\\ \times\ 10\end{array}$	$\begin{array}{r}7\\ \times\ 5\end{array}$	$\begin{array}{r}9\\ \times\ 6\end{array}$	$\begin{array}{r}4\\ \times\ 10\end{array}$	$\begin{array}{r}9\\ \times\ 4\end{array}$	$\begin{array}{r}11\\ \times\ 7\end{array}$	$\begin{array}{r}11\\ \times\ 1\end{array}$	$\begin{array}{r}8\\ \times\ 12\end{array}$
$\begin{array}{r}3\\ \times\ 8\end{array}$	$\begin{array}{r}10\\ \times\ 9\end{array}$	$\begin{array}{r}5\\ \times\ 8\end{array}$	$\begin{array}{r}6\\ \times\ 9\end{array}$	$\begin{array}{r}11\\ \times\ 3\end{array}$	$\begin{array}{r}1\\ \times\ 9\end{array}$	$\begin{array}{r}1\\ \times\ 11\end{array}$	$\begin{array}{r}1\\ \times\ 5\end{array}$	$\begin{array}{r}7\\ \times\ 6\end{array}$	$\begin{array}{r}1\\ \times\ 3\end{array}$
$\begin{array}{r}3\\ \times\ 12\end{array}$	$\begin{array}{r}7\\ \times\ 12\end{array}$	$\begin{array}{r}1\\ \times\ 4\end{array}$	$\begin{array}{r}10\\ \times\ 3\end{array}$	$\begin{array}{r}11\\ \times\ 4\end{array}$	$\begin{array}{r}11\\ \times\ 9\end{array}$	$\begin{array}{r}5\\ \times\ 2\end{array}$	$\begin{array}{r}1\\ \times\ 12\end{array}$	$\begin{array}{r}5\\ \times\ 1\end{array}$	$\begin{array}{r}0\\ \times\ 8\end{array}$
$\begin{array}{r}6\\ \times\ 6\end{array}$	$\begin{array}{r}3\\ \times\ 5\end{array}$	$\begin{array}{r}2\\ \times\ 8\end{array}$	$\begin{array}{r}6\\ \times\ 11\end{array}$	$\begin{array}{r}9\\ \times\ 1\end{array}$	$\begin{array}{r}0\\ \times\ 7\end{array}$	$\begin{array}{r}10\\ \times\ 11\end{array}$	$\begin{array}{r}3\\ \times\ 6\end{array}$	$\begin{array}{r}2\\ \times\ 10\end{array}$	$\begin{array}{r}11\\ \times\ 0\end{array}$
$\begin{array}{r}8\\ \times\ 8\end{array}$	$\begin{array}{r}12\\ \times\ 7\end{array}$	$\begin{array}{r}2\\ \times\ 11\end{array}$	$\begin{array}{r}9\\ \times\ 5\end{array}$	$\begin{array}{r}10\\ \times\ 5\end{array}$	$\begin{array}{r}4\\ \times\ 3\end{array}$	$\begin{array}{r}9\\ \times\ 10\end{array}$	$\begin{array}{r}6\\ \times\ 8\end{array}$	$\begin{array}{r}3\\ \times\ 4\end{array}$	$\begin{array}{r}7\\ \times\ 4\end{array}$

6 × 6	0 × 3	3 × 3	8 × 4	12 × 0	10 × 9	7 × 0	4 × 3	10 × 6	0 × 10
5 × 11	10 × 3	11 × 4	11 × 2	5 × 2	3 × 4	7 × 2	9 × 7	12 × 11	11 × 7
3 × 8	1 × 2	9 × 4	0 × 6	2 × 12	8 × 1	7 × 1	7 × 5	2 × 3	9 × 5
4 × 8	4 × 5	12 × 9	1 × 1	7 × 7	1 × 5	4 × 6	1 × 10	8 × 12	0 × 7
9 × 8	4 × 4	2 × 5	10 × 8	0 × 12	6 × 11	2 × 1	3 × 10	12 × 4	6 × 12
3 × 6	8 × 5	12 × 1	3 × 2	9 × 1	4 × 0	6 × 3	0 × 9	5 × 12	8 × 7
8 × 8	2 × 11	11 × 6	0 × 2	10 × 0	7 × 12	4 × 7	1 × 6	11 × 9	6 × 7
10 × 10	1 × 0	7 × 9	6 × 4	11 × 8	2 × 7	11 × 5	2 × 8	12 × 5	2 × 6
1 × 9	2 × 2	10 × 7	4 × 1	5 × 10	8 × 10	2 × 4	5 × 9	0 × 11	11 × 0
12 × 3	7 × 10	9 × 3	3 × 5	10 × 11	5 × 6	0 × 8	9 × 9	10 × 1	11 × 10

Name _____   Date _____

6 × 0	10 × 9	11 × 10	0 × 1	3 × 4	0 × 12	11 × 4	1 × 1	3 × 11	12 × 0
4 × 1	3 × 10	4 × 4	7 × 2	0 × 8	4 × 12	8 × 10	7 × 5	2 × 9	9 × 7
8 × 3	9 × 1	3 × 3	6 × 12	2 × 8	9 × 9	12 × 4	7 × 6	12 × 12	11 × 11
3 × 0	2 × 7	10 × 11	10 × 4	9 × 5	1 × 7	2 × 3	6 × 9	12 × 2	5 × 5
9 × 12	2 × 4	8 × 0	0 × 0	4 × 5	7 × 4	0 × 9	8 × 6	10 × 2	3 × 12
5 × 7	4 × 0	3 × 9	0 × 10	1 × 8	9 × 6	6 × 11	2 × 10	0 × 4	5 × 2
8 × 7	9 × 11	10 × 8	12 × 1	12 × 7	2 × 1	0 × 7	5 × 12	2 × 6	11 × 0
5 × 0	1 × 2	7 × 9	7 × 11	0 × 3	8 × 9	1 × 3	11 × 3	12 × 8	7 × 12
5 × 11	1 × 0	5 × 8	8 × 8	11 × 1	4 × 9	6 × 5	4 × 11	2 × 0	11 × 12
10 × 6	8 × 1	9 × 2	11 × 8	2 × 12	2 × 2	11 × 7	12 × 6	8 × 2	9 × 4

Name _____ Date _____

0 × 9	0 × 2	9 × 2	0 × 1	8 × 9	1 × 8	10 × 2	1 × 12	12 × 6	2 × 1
6 × 0	7 × 3	6 × 1	5 × 0	4 × 2	10 × 4	12 × 1	7 × 6	2 × 2	7 × 1
11 × 1	0 × 6	9 × 4	6 × 2	6 × 4	6 × 6	4 × 9	1 × 6	1 × 9	12 × 9
8 × 12	3 × 9	8 × 6	11 × 5	8 × 4	0 × 7	12 × 5	10 × 8	0 × 12	4 × 0
1 × 7	7 × 4	11 × 9	3 × 4	12 × 8	1 × 1	4 × 4	10 × 3	7 × 2	0 × 11
5 × 3	2 × 0	5 × 4	5 × 12	3 × 2	11 × 10	7 × 5	2 × 4	12 × 4	9 × 11
8 × 8	3 × 1	7 × 7	3 × 5	8 × 0	12 × 10	4 × 3	4 × 11	2 × 8	6 × 5
0 × 5	11 × 8	7 × 11	9 × 12	6 × 8	9 × 8	5 × 9	5 × 6	4 × 5	11 × 6
10 × 0	5 × 5	8 × 3	11 × 7	5 × 8	11 × 3	5 × 2	6 × 12	10 × 1	12 × 0
2 × 10	1 × 0	0 × 4	9 × 5	1 × 4	10 × 11	6 × 11	3 × 11	9 × 10	3 × 7

Name _____   Date _____

6 × 4	0 × 0	4 × 6	6 × 3	4 × 9	8 × 5	9 × 8	5 × 3	9 × 3	2 × 5
5 × 7	10 × 12	6 × 0	11 × 0	6 × 8	9 × 2	0 × 6	1 × 10	5 × 6	12 × 8
9 × 10	0 × 3	6 × 12	0 × 12	2 × 1	9 × 9	10 × 2	2 × 2	10 × 8	8 × 1
12 × 9	10 × 3	0 × 9	11 × 8	2 × 10	3 × 1	4 × 5	8 × 9	12 × 10	1 × 6
11 × 3	5 × 1	12 × 1	11 × 12	3 × 4	6 × 10	5 × 12	7 × 11	8 × 8	4 × 10
5 × 8	7 × 6	11 × 7	10 × 10	6 × 9	9 × 0	9 × 4	10 × 0	12 × 6	8 × 3
7 × 4	7 × 0	2 × 3	12 × 2	7 × 9	6 × 5	12 × 5	10 × 9	1 × 12	3 × 10
5 × 2	3 × 9	2 × 7	3 × 6	0 × 2	9 × 7	4 × 2	0 × 8	1 × 0	2 × 11
0 × 10	6 × 1	7 × 5	6 × 11	10 × 4	9 × 12	1 × 1	3 × 0	7 × 12	1 × 4
12 × 4	8 × 2	9 × 11	4 × 1	2 × 8	1 × 2	9 × 6	9 × 5	2 × 6	4 × 8

$\begin{array}{r}0\\ \times\,10\\ \hline\end{array}$	$\begin{array}{r}0\\ \times\,9\\ \hline\end{array}$	$\begin{array}{r}11\\ \times\,12\\ \hline\end{array}$	$\begin{array}{r}0\\ \times\,8\\ \hline\end{array}$	$\begin{array}{r}1\\ \times\,1\\ \hline\end{array}$	$\begin{array}{r}10\\ \times\,6\\ \hline\end{array}$	$\begin{array}{r}11\\ \times\,11\\ \hline\end{array}$	$\begin{array}{r}1\\ \times\,6\\ \hline\end{array}$	$\begin{array}{r}11\\ \times\,8\\ \hline\end{array}$	$\begin{array}{r}6\\ \times\,7\\ \hline\end{array}$
$\begin{array}{r}0\\ \times\,1\\ \hline\end{array}$	$\begin{array}{r}5\\ \times\,1\\ \hline\end{array}$	$\begin{array}{r}9\\ \times\,2\\ \hline\end{array}$	$\begin{array}{r}2\\ \times\,11\\ \hline\end{array}$	$\begin{array}{r}0\\ \times\,6\\ \hline\end{array}$	$\begin{array}{r}9\\ \times\,5\\ \hline\end{array}$	$\begin{array}{r}9\\ \times\,3\\ \hline\end{array}$	$\begin{array}{r}6\\ \times\,2\\ \hline\end{array}$	$\begin{array}{r}9\\ \times\,10\\ \hline\end{array}$	$\begin{array}{r}2\\ \times\,3\\ \hline\end{array}$
$\begin{array}{r}10\\ \times\,1\\ \hline\end{array}$	$\begin{array}{r}11\\ \times\,0\\ \hline\end{array}$	$\begin{array}{r}10\\ \times\,12\\ \hline\end{array}$	$\begin{array}{r}9\\ \times\,11\\ \hline\end{array}$	$\begin{array}{r}2\\ \times\,6\\ \hline\end{array}$	$\begin{array}{r}8\\ \times\,6\\ \hline\end{array}$	$\begin{array}{r}9\\ \times\,1\\ \hline\end{array}$	$\begin{array}{r}7\\ \times\,4\\ \hline\end{array}$	$\begin{array}{r}7\\ \times\,9\\ \hline\end{array}$	$\begin{array}{r}6\\ \times\,8\\ \hline\end{array}$
$\begin{array}{r}0\\ \times\,12\\ \hline\end{array}$	$\begin{array}{r}9\\ \times\,4\\ \hline\end{array}$	$\begin{array}{r}7\\ \times\,2\\ \hline\end{array}$	$\begin{array}{r}1\\ \times\,2\\ \hline\end{array}$	$\begin{array}{r}6\\ \times\,4\\ \hline\end{array}$	$\begin{array}{r}8\\ \times\,4\\ \hline\end{array}$	$\begin{array}{r}7\\ \times\,3\\ \hline\end{array}$	$\begin{array}{r}4\\ \times\,8\\ \hline\end{array}$	$\begin{array}{r}6\\ \times\,6\\ \hline\end{array}$	$\begin{array}{r}3\\ \times\,10\\ \hline\end{array}$
$\begin{array}{r}0\\ \times\,5\\ \hline\end{array}$	$\begin{array}{r}0\\ \times\,4\\ \hline\end{array}$	$\begin{array}{r}12\\ \times\,2\\ \hline\end{array}$	$\begin{array}{r}4\\ \times\,3\\ \hline\end{array}$	$\begin{array}{r}6\\ \times\,3\\ \hline\end{array}$	$\begin{array}{r}3\\ \times\,7\\ \hline\end{array}$	$\begin{array}{r}1\\ \times\,12\\ \hline\end{array}$	$\begin{array}{r}4\\ \times\,10\\ \hline\end{array}$	$\begin{array}{r}10\\ \times\,5\\ \hline\end{array}$	$\begin{array}{r}5\\ \times\,5\\ \hline\end{array}$
$\begin{array}{r}7\\ \times\,0\\ \hline\end{array}$	$\begin{array}{r}2\\ \times\,4\\ \hline\end{array}$	$\begin{array}{r}8\\ \times\,12\\ \hline\end{array}$	$\begin{array}{r}2\\ \times\,2\\ \hline\end{array}$	$\begin{array}{r}10\\ \times\,0\\ \hline\end{array}$	$\begin{array}{r}7\\ \times\,11\\ \hline\end{array}$	$\begin{array}{r}11\\ \times\,2\\ \hline\end{array}$	$\begin{array}{r}7\\ \times\,7\\ \hline\end{array}$	$\begin{array}{r}6\\ \times\,10\\ \hline\end{array}$	$\begin{array}{r}6\\ \times\,9\\ \hline\end{array}$
$\begin{array}{r}12\\ \times\,6\\ \hline\end{array}$	$\begin{array}{r}2\\ \times\,7\\ \hline\end{array}$	$\begin{array}{r}10\\ \times\,9\\ \hline\end{array}$	$\begin{array}{r}5\\ \times\,8\\ \hline\end{array}$	$\begin{array}{r}1\\ \times\,4\\ \hline\end{array}$	$\begin{array}{r}2\\ \times\,12\\ \hline\end{array}$	$\begin{array}{r}1\\ \times\,0\\ \hline\end{array}$	$\begin{array}{r}3\\ \times\,5\\ \hline\end{array}$	$\begin{array}{r}8\\ \times\,11\\ \hline\end{array}$	$\begin{array}{r}12\\ \times\,3\\ \hline\end{array}$
$\begin{array}{r}11\\ \times\,4\\ \hline\end{array}$	$\begin{array}{r}4\\ \times\,6\\ \hline\end{array}$	$\begin{array}{r}5\\ \times\,0\\ \hline\end{array}$	$\begin{array}{r}10\\ \times\,7\\ \hline\end{array}$	$\begin{array}{r}6\\ \times\,0\\ \hline\end{array}$	$\begin{array}{r}9\\ \times\,8\\ \hline\end{array}$	$\begin{array}{r}6\\ \times\,1\\ \hline\end{array}$	$\begin{array}{r}12\\ \times\,4\\ \hline\end{array}$	$\begin{array}{r}5\\ \times\,3\\ \hline\end{array}$	$\begin{array}{r}2\\ \times\,8\\ \hline\end{array}$
$\begin{array}{r}11\\ \times\,6\\ \hline\end{array}$	$\begin{array}{r}4\\ \times\,5\\ \hline\end{array}$	$\begin{array}{r}4\\ \times\,7\\ \hline\end{array}$	$\begin{array}{r}2\\ \times\,5\\ \hline\end{array}$	$\begin{array}{r}11\\ \times\,3\\ \hline\end{array}$	$\begin{array}{r}5\\ \times\,6\\ \hline\end{array}$	$\begin{array}{r}5\\ \times\,9\\ \hline\end{array}$	$\begin{array}{r}3\\ \times\,9\\ \hline\end{array}$	$\begin{array}{r}12\\ \times\,8\\ \hline\end{array}$	$\begin{array}{r}0\\ \times\,7\\ \hline\end{array}$
$\begin{array}{r}8\\ \times\,9\\ \hline\end{array}$	$\begin{array}{r}9\\ \times\,0\\ \hline\end{array}$	$\begin{array}{r}5\\ \times\,7\\ \hline\end{array}$	$\begin{array}{r}11\\ \times\,7\\ \hline\end{array}$	$\begin{array}{r}12\\ \times\,1\\ \hline\end{array}$	$\begin{array}{r}11\\ \times\,9\\ \hline\end{array}$	$\begin{array}{r}7\\ \times\,10\\ \hline\end{array}$	$\begin{array}{r}3\\ \times\,12\\ \hline\end{array}$	$\begin{array}{r}8\\ \times\,3\\ \hline\end{array}$	$\begin{array}{r}9\\ \times\,12\\ \hline\end{array}$

Name _____   Date _____

2 × 1	0 × 3	2 × 2	3 × 1	4 × 1	2 × 12	9 × 6	5 × 4	4 × 12	6 × 11
2 × 9	2 × 8	9 × 0	9 × 9	6 × 3	4 × 11	4 × 2	0 × 9	1 × 5	3 × 4
5 × 12	3 × 8	11 × 7	5 × 7	6 × 0	2 × 3	8 × 12	9 × 7	10 × 12	0 × 11
7 × 4	7 × 6	12 × 5	8 × 11	5 × 8	4 × 7	0 × 5	7 × 12	5 × 6	8 × 0
6 × 4	12 × 1	7 × 10	0 × 10	0 × 1	2 × 5	9 × 8	3 × 6	1 × 10	8 × 7
1 × 12	1 × 9	1 × 2	8 × 4	11 × 1	5 × 3	6 × 1	0 × 7	11 × 5	4 × 4
9 × 10	6 × 5	5 × 0	11 × 8	1 × 11	10 × 9	9 × 2	0 × 0	5 × 10	4 × 9
12 × 10	12 × 2	12 × 8	8 × 8	8 × 6	7 × 9	10 × 5	4 × 0	2 × 0	11 × 0
10 × 6	7 × 11	5 × 11	4 × 8	3 × 7	12 × 12	7 × 8	1 × 0	6 × 12	0 × 2
8 × 3	9 × 1	12 × 4	8 × 10	0 × 4	3 × 3	3 × 5	7 × 0	6 × 2	5 × 5

Name _____ Date _____

0 × 5	3 × 3	2 × 9	3 × 1	2 × 1	10 × 0	3 × 0	2 × 7	7 × 3	3 × 8
6 × 11	6 × 7	4 × 3	9 × 11	8 × 9	6 × 1	5 × 12	8 × 8	8 × 1	3 × 4
10 × 1	9 × 3	5 × 7	1 × 9	6 × 4	9 × 2	8 × 2	7 × 1	2 × 3	9 × 4
1 × 11	6 × 9	11 × 12	11 × 1	1 × 3	5 × 8	5 × 0	10 × 7	6 × 6	8 × 3
0 × 6	7 × 6	10 × 5	4 × 9	12 × 0	1 × 5	7 × 11	7 × 12	12 × 4	6 × 12
12 × 8	6 × 0	11 × 6	6 × 3	10 × 8	4 × 0	6 × 2	0 × 8	2 × 4	12 × 5
11 × 0	8 × 4	3 × 2	12 × 6	0 × 10	10 × 11	0 × 7	9 × 0	11 × 9	5 × 9
7 × 4	9 × 9	4 × 5	4 × 6	8 × 11	4 × 10	10 × 3	11 × 2	0 × 4	5 × 6
7 × 5	3 × 12	10 × 4	11 × 3	9 × 6	11 × 5	7 × 9	3 × 9	9 × 1	7 × 8
10 × 9	12 × 7	5 × 5	5 × 3	1 × 1	12 × 9	0 × 0	5 × 10	2 × 8	10 × 12

Name _____ Date _____

9 × 2	5 × 2	3 × 3	0 × 5	12 × 1	8 × 1	1 × 0	10 × 5	8 × 7	7 × 0
5 × 4	6 × 6	1 × 11	7 × 8	8 × 2	11 × 0	3 × 9	0 × 3	9 × 5	6 × 1
8 × 3	1 × 5	6 × 11	7 × 3	7 × 6	6 × 4	1 × 9	4 × 12	10 × 9	11 × 6
2 × 7	5 × 5	10 × 3	4 × 6	1 × 4	0 × 11	8 × 8	11 × 2	1 × 1	3 × 7
3 × 6	11 × 9	3 × 4	8 × 6	1 × 7	6 × 9	11 × 5	8 × 4	9 × 6	5 × 0
4 × 9	1 × 6	7 × 11	0 × 1	1 × 2	0 × 7	2 × 11	9 × 8	10 × 4	9 × 7
0 × 9	2 × 2	7 × 10	6 × 7	11 × 10	3 × 2	12 × 7	5 × 9	2 × 0	0 × 4
10 × 12	8 × 0	0 × 6	12 × 10	7 × 4	9 × 12	8 × 12	9 × 9	10 × 6	1 × 10
2 × 3	6 × 3	5 × 6	12 × 5	1 × 8	2 × 1	10 × 10	11 × 12	3 × 12	3 × 10
4 × 1	10 × 8	12 × 3	7 × 5	4 × 2	11 × 11	9 × 10	6 × 8	7 × 12	2 × 8

Name _____   Date _____

2 × 2	11 × 1	4 × 1	5 × 1	6 × 4	7 × 8	6 × 5	12 × 5	10 × 8	2 × 4
3 × 11	1 × 5	1 × 3	10 × 10	12 × 3	10 × 1	10 × 11	7 × 7	8 × 7	0 × 7
3 × 4	6 × 2	3 × 9	4 × 10	5 × 5	5 × 6	8 × 0	7 × 9	11 × 7	9 × 1
10 × 0	4 × 5	9 × 9	4 × 6	6 × 12	8 × 6	5 × 2	1 × 7	0 × 11	9 × 6
5 × 9	7 × 4	6 × 3	10 × 9	2 × 11	9 × 3	3 × 8	12 × 2	6 × 0	1 × 6
0 × 4	2 × 3	6 × 1	0 × 5	11 × 6	6 × 7	1 × 4	9 × 8	5 × 7	4 × 8
10 × 6	6 × 8	4 × 9	1 × 2	3 × 10	7 × 1	12 × 4	0 × 6	3 × 3	2 × 8
1 × 10	0 × 1	11 × 0	3 × 5	3 × 6	5 × 12	8 × 12	12 × 9	10 × 2	7 × 6
8 × 9	7 × 3	5 × 11	11 × 2	12 × 0	5 × 0	8 × 3	0 × 0	8 × 5	8 × 10
6 × 9	4 × 7	7 × 2	9 × 10	9 × 0	8 × 4	12 × 7	3 × 7	8 × 1	5 × 4

Name _____ Date _____

6 × 10	6 × 7	12 × 7	0 × 2	0 × 3	10 × 5	3 × 3	12 × 9	3 × 1	2 × 6
3 × 5	6 × 3	10 × 1	6 × 8	11 × 8	1 × 6	6 × 2	10 × 10	3 × 11	2 × 10
3 × 6	6 × 6	4 × 3	11 × 0	8 × 6	7 × 4	6 × 5	8 × 9	10 × 8	1 × 2
11 × 9	6 × 11	7 × 12	7 × 0	9 × 2	4 × 4	7 × 5	4 × 7	1 × 0	3 × 7
8 × 0	1 × 4	5 × 2	9 × 5	1 × 7	10 × 9	3 × 4	10 × 3	7 × 10	4 × 9
4 × 5	5 × 8	10 × 2	12 × 1	9 × 4	5 × 3	0 × 11	0 × 8	12 × 10	6 × 1
10 × 6	2 × 9	11 × 4	7 × 7	9 × 7	11 × 6	6 × 4	4 × 2	9 × 6	8 × 5
9 × 11	1 × 11	11 × 5	5 × 4	8 × 10	3 × 8	0 × 1	5 × 12	0 × 7	7 × 8
12 × 6	12 × 4	5 × 5	9 × 3	3 × 10	4 × 12	9 × 1	1 × 10	3 × 2	12 × 2
6 × 0	1 × 3	7 × 1	2 × 11	11 × 7	12 × 8	1 × 8	7 × 11	4 × 8	7 × 6

Name _____ Date _____

2 × 4	1 × 5	3 × 3	10 × 6	2 × 0	6 × 3	3 × 8	5 × 0	10 × 1	4 × 12
9 × 8	12 × 7	2 × 10	10 × 0	5 × 4	9 × 4	5 × 10	12 × 1	12 × 3	3 × 0
6 × 4	9 × 0	9 × 1	1 × 12	4 × 11	5 × 2	7 × 0	0 × 12	7 × 1	7 × 8
11 × 9	6 × 11	2 × 2	8 × 0	9 × 3	3 × 9	12 × 9	1 × 7	9 × 5	11 × 12
8 × 1	10 × 8	10 × 11	10 × 10	11 × 0	2 × 8	4 × 9	3 × 2	8 × 12	5 × 8
11 × 10	9 × 9	4 × 5	1 × 4	1 × 6	10 × 12	8 × 9	8 × 8	2 × 5	6 × 0
2 × 12	0 × 9	6 × 7	2 × 11	4 × 4	10 × 5	1 × 8	0 × 10	7 × 7	1 × 0
8 × 5	5 × 11	7 × 12	12 × 6	7 × 3	8 × 11	8 × 6	12 × 5	0 × 7	0 × 1
10 × 9	0 × 0	10 × 4	5 × 7	2 × 3	0 × 8	2 × 7	11 × 4	10 × 7	1 × 10
0 × 5	6 × 9	9 × 12	2 × 6	1 × 11	6 × 6	6 × 8	12 × 2	7 × 5	11 × 2

Name _____   Date _____

4 × 7	7 × 11	8 × 0	8 × 2	9 × 9	1 × 9	3 × 6	2 × 1	5 × 4	1 × 8
10 × 4	7 × 2	4 × 9	9 × 11	10 × 2	11 × 1	10 × 3	8 × 8	9 × 1	1 × 0
0 × 5	11 × 8	9 × 12	7 × 7	0 × 0	10 × 7	2 × 6	7 × 4	1 × 1	7 × 5
11 × 2	0 × 7	11 × 7	0 × 4	12 × 1	2 × 12	4 × 3	8 × 7	10 × 1	10 × 6
7 × 8	5 × 7	4 × 10	8 × 1	8 × 11	9 × 5	5 × 2	2 × 0	3 × 3	6 × 7
6 × 0	2 × 5	3 × 1	3 × 12	2 × 2	4 × 11	3 × 11	0 × 12	3 × 5	10 × 0
6 × 6	9 × 8	2 × 4	4 × 6	3 × 2	2 × 8	10 × 8	9 × 6	8 × 4	12 × 8
5 × 6	12 × 10	9 × 4	12 × 6	9 × 0	6 × 10	1 × 7	7 × 12	0 × 6	4 × 0
12 × 2	12 × 5	2 × 7	8 × 12	10 × 11	6 × 9	4 × 5	6 × 11	5 × 12	11 × 12
4 × 2	3 × 9	5 × 11	2 × 11	5 × 3	4 × 12	5 × 1	11 × 0	1 × 10	9 × 10

Name _____   Date _____

18 ÷ 6 =	28 ÷ 7 =	20 ÷ 2 =	56 ÷ 8 =	10 ÷ 5 =
10 ÷ 1 =	144 ÷ 12 =	9 ÷ 9 =	16 ÷ 8 =	0 ÷ 4 =
4 ÷ 2 =	40 ÷ 4 =	18 ÷ 2 =	70 ÷ 10 =	36 ÷ 12 =
10 ÷ 10 =	120 ÷ 12 =	40 ÷ 10 =	3 ÷ 1 =	2 ÷ 1 =
0 ÷ 9 =	25 ÷ 5 =	110 ÷ 11 =	15 ÷ 3 =	30 ÷ 10 =
20 ÷ 4 =	99 ÷ 11 =	9 ÷ 3 =	24 ÷ 4 =	50 ÷ 10 =
35 ÷ 7 =	70 ÷ 7 =	28 ÷ 4 =	27 ÷ 9 =	24 ÷ 2 =
88 ÷ 11 =	0 ÷ 5 =	7 ÷ 1 =	24 ÷ 3 =	50 ÷ 5 =
9 ÷ 1 =	54 ÷ 9 =	121 ÷ 11 =	12 ÷ 12 =	45 ÷ 5 =
90 ÷ 10 =	5 ÷ 5 =	42 ÷ 7 =	0 ÷ 8 =	30 ÷ 5 =
35 ÷ 5 =	5 ÷ 1 =	8 ÷ 4 =	108 ÷ 12 =	0 ÷ 6 =
15 ÷ 5 =	72 ÷ 12 =	8 ÷ 1 =	12 ÷ 6 =	96 ÷ 12 =
132 ÷ 11 =	40 ÷ 5 =	80 ÷ 8 =	6 ÷ 3 =	64 ÷ 8 =
4 ÷ 4 =	18 ÷ 9 =	36 ÷ 6 =	32 ÷ 4 =	110 ÷ 10 =
66 ÷ 11 =	12 ÷ 3 =	21 ÷ 7 =	44 ÷ 11 =	8 ÷ 8 =
24 ÷ 8 =	40 ÷ 8 =	44 ÷ 4 =	22 ÷ 11 =	12 ÷ 1 =
4 ÷ 1 =	108 ÷ 9 =	22 ÷ 2 =	36 ÷ 4 =	30 ÷ 6 =
63 ÷ 9 =	63 ÷ 7 =	21 ÷ 3 =	14 ÷ 2 =	16 ÷ 4 =
10 ÷ 2 =	48 ÷ 6 =	90 ÷ 9 =	80 ÷ 10 =	54 ÷ 6 =
132 ÷ 12 =	96 ÷ 8 =	11 ÷ 11 =	99 ÷ 9 =	24 ÷ 6 =

Name _____ Date _____

16 ÷ 4 =	8 ÷ 8 =	20 ÷ 5 =	9 ÷ 1 =	9 ÷ 9 =
66 ÷ 11 =	0 ÷ 7 =	32 ÷ 4 =	0 ÷ 4 =	5 ÷ 1 =
22 ÷ 2 =	108 ÷ 12 =	8 ÷ 2 =	24 ÷ 2 =	10 ÷ 2 =
6 ÷ 1 =	6 ÷ 6 =	40 ÷ 4 =	24 ÷ 6 =	36 ÷ 3 =
55 ÷ 11 =	88 ÷ 11 =	50 ÷ 10 =	36 ÷ 4 =	96 ÷ 12 =
5 ÷ 5 =	63 ÷ 7 =	18 ÷ 6 =	60 ÷ 10 =	54 ÷ 9 =
12 ÷ 4 =	35 ÷ 7 =	15 ÷ 3 =	40 ÷ 5 =	48 ÷ 6 =
0 ÷ 9 =	0 ÷ 10 =	21 ÷ 7 =	63 ÷ 9 =	0 ÷ 5 =
24 ÷ 12 =	18 ÷ 3 =	70 ÷ 7 =	4 ÷ 1 =	24 ÷ 8 =
33 ÷ 11 =	49 ÷ 7 =	14 ÷ 2 =	4 ÷ 2 =	10 ÷ 10 =
66 ÷ 6 =	84 ÷ 7 =	2 ÷ 2 =	120 ÷ 10 =	7 ÷ 7 =
30 ÷ 6 =	40 ÷ 10 =	20 ÷ 4 =	24 ÷ 4 =	3 ÷ 1 =
88 ÷ 8 =	8 ÷ 1 =	3 ÷ 3 =	55 ÷ 5 =	50 ÷ 5 =
84 ÷ 12 =	132 ÷ 11 =	12 ÷ 6 =	4 ÷ 4 =	10 ÷ 1 =
90 ÷ 9 =	42 ÷ 7 =	72 ÷ 12 =	99 ÷ 9 =	77 ÷ 11 =
9 ÷ 3 =	0 ÷ 2 =	30 ÷ 10 =	21 ÷ 3 =	27 ÷ 3 =
20 ÷ 10 =	28 ÷ 4 =	81 ÷ 9 =	27 ÷ 9 =	6 ÷ 2 =
0 ÷ 3 =	28 ÷ 7 =	16 ÷ 2 =	25 ÷ 5 =	48 ÷ 4 =
54 ÷ 6 =	0 ÷ 12 =	0 ÷ 11 =	7 ÷ 1 =	0 ÷ 8 =
18 ÷ 9 =	110 ÷ 11 =	6 ÷ 3 =	45 ÷ 9 =	12 ÷ 3 =

0 ÷ 3 =	4 ÷ 4 =	81 ÷ 9 =	88 ÷ 8 =	44 ÷ 4 =
28 ÷ 4 =	10 ÷ 10 =	2 ÷ 1 =	84 ÷ 12 =	77 ÷ 11 =
36 ÷ 9 =	36 ÷ 12 =	10 ÷ 1 =	55 ÷ 11 =	11 ÷ 1 =
60 ÷ 12 =	33 ÷ 11 =	30 ÷ 10 =	56 ÷ 7 =	72 ÷ 9 =
20 ÷ 5 =	22 ÷ 2 =	40 ÷ 4 =	4 ÷ 1 =	9 ÷ 9 =
12 ÷ 4 =	10 ÷ 5 =	12 ÷ 6 =	6 ÷ 1 =	49 ÷ 7 =
0 ÷ 4 =	36 ÷ 6 =	15 ÷ 3 =	44 ÷ 11 =	12 ÷ 2 =
5 ÷ 1 =	99 ÷ 9 =	24 ÷ 12 =	24 ÷ 3 =	70 ÷ 7 =
64 ÷ 8 =	50 ÷ 10 =	16 ÷ 4 =	66 ÷ 11 =	35 ÷ 7 =
60 ÷ 6 =	22 ÷ 11 =	0 ÷ 11 =	11 ÷ 11 =	18 ÷ 6 =
48 ÷ 12 =	12 ÷ 1 =	9 ÷ 1 =	72 ÷ 12 =	72 ÷ 8 =
6 ÷ 6 =	66 ÷ 6 =	108 ÷ 9 =	14 ÷ 7 =	16 ÷ 2 =
10 ÷ 2 =	72 ÷ 6 =	24 ÷ 8 =	1 ÷ 1 =	27 ÷ 9 =
54 ÷ 6 =	30 ÷ 5 =	4 ÷ 2 =	90 ÷ 9 =	99 ÷ 11 =
3 ÷ 3 =	21 ÷ 3 =	55 ÷ 5 =	14 ÷ 2 =	2 ÷ 2 =
77 ÷ 7 =	90 ÷ 10 =	45 ÷ 5 =	30 ÷ 3 =	80 ÷ 8 =
18 ÷ 9 =	110 ÷ 11 =	56 ÷ 8 =	80 ÷ 10 =	8 ÷ 4 =
15 ÷ 5 =	54 ÷ 9 =	132 ÷ 11 =	24 ÷ 6 =	24 ÷ 4 =
0 ÷ 6 =	110 ÷ 10 =	30 ÷ 6 =	25 ÷ 5 =	0 ÷ 5 =
42 ÷ 7 =	16 ÷ 8 =	40 ÷ 8 =	0 ÷ 1 =	60 ÷ 10 =

20 ÷ 10 =	12 ÷ 12 =	8 ÷ 4 =	7 ÷ 1 =	18 ÷ 6 =
63 ÷ 7 =	84 ÷ 12 =	18 ÷ 3 =	10 ÷ 2 =	27 ÷ 9 =
88 ÷ 8 =	32 ÷ 8 =	40 ÷ 5 =	4 ÷ 1 =	3 ÷ 1 =
30 ÷ 5 =	11 ÷ 11 =	0 ÷ 5 =	64 ÷ 8 =	144 ÷ 12 =
24 ÷ 4 =	132 ÷ 12 =	6 ÷ 6 =	10 ÷ 10 =	70 ÷ 7 =
55 ÷ 5 =	12 ÷ 2 =	16 ÷ 8 =	88 ÷ 11 =	50 ÷ 10 =
36 ÷ 6 =	1 ÷ 1 =	22 ÷ 11 =	77 ÷ 11 =	60 ÷ 5 =
24 ÷ 6 =	84 ÷ 7 =	54 ÷ 6 =	96 ÷ 12 =	2 ÷ 2 =
14 ÷ 7 =	4 ÷ 4 =	66 ÷ 11 =	36 ÷ 3 =	108 ÷ 9 =
72 ÷ 8 =	0 ÷ 12 =	8 ÷ 8 =	22 ÷ 2 =	0 ÷ 11 =
20 ÷ 5 =	48 ÷ 8 =	9 ÷ 9 =	25 ÷ 5 =	42 ÷ 7 =
30 ÷ 10 =	35 ÷ 7 =	60 ÷ 10 =	15 ÷ 5 =	36 ÷ 4 =
14 ÷ 2 =	72 ÷ 12 =	6 ÷ 1 =	90 ÷ 10 =	55 ÷ 11 =
8 ÷ 1 =	5 ÷ 1 =	21 ÷ 7 =	0 ÷ 8 =	44 ÷ 11 =
12 ÷ 6 =	11 ÷ 1 =	6 ÷ 2 =	33 ÷ 11 =	0 ÷ 9 =
2 ÷ 1 =	3 ÷ 3 =	44 ÷ 4 =	120 ÷ 10 =	81 ÷ 9 =
4 ÷ 2 =	66 ÷ 6 =	0 ÷ 4 =	110 ÷ 10 =	32 ÷ 4 =
0 ÷ 3 =	48 ÷ 4 =	0 ÷ 10 =	9 ÷ 3 =	35 ÷ 5 =
36 ÷ 9 =	7 ÷ 7 =	80 ÷ 10 =	5 ÷ 5 =	90 ÷ 9 =
12 ÷ 4 =	77 ÷ 7 =	70 ÷ 10 =	54 ÷ 9 =	120 ÷ 12 =

Name _____   Date _____

9 ÷ 3 =	4 ÷ 4 =	90 ÷ 10 =	40 ÷ 5 =	0 ÷ 12 =
55 ÷ 11 =	4 ÷ 1 =	24 ÷ 12 =	63 ÷ 9 =	54 ÷ 6 =
6 ÷ 3 =	20 ÷ 5 =	96 ÷ 12 =	22 ÷ 2 =	60 ÷ 6 =
144 ÷ 12 =	30 ÷ 6 =	80 ÷ 8 =	0 ÷ 3 =	0 ÷ 10 =
36 ÷ 4 =	48 ÷ 8 =	3 ÷ 3 =	72 ÷ 9 =	7 ÷ 1 =
36 ÷ 3 =	27 ÷ 9 =	32 ÷ 4 =	16 ÷ 8 =	63 ÷ 7 =
84 ÷ 12 =	15 ÷ 5 =	110 ÷ 11 =	30 ÷ 5 =	99 ÷ 9 =
18 ÷ 9 =	45 ÷ 5 =	49 ÷ 7 =	0 ÷ 7 =	56 ÷ 7 =
18 ÷ 6 =	28 ÷ 4 =	55 ÷ 5 =	66 ÷ 11 =	16 ÷ 4 =
40 ÷ 10 =	80 ÷ 10 =	45 ÷ 9 =	12 ÷ 2 =	6 ÷ 2 =
9 ÷ 1 =	12 ÷ 4 =	0 ÷ 9 =	81 ÷ 9 =	8 ÷ 1 =
60 ÷ 12 =	99 ÷ 11 =	84 ÷ 7 =	96 ÷ 8 =	12 ÷ 1 =
5 ÷ 1 =	28 ÷ 7 =	24 ÷ 6 =	33 ÷ 3 =	24 ÷ 8 =
10 ÷ 1 =	27 ÷ 3 =	5 ÷ 5 =	9 ÷ 9 =	25 ÷ 5 =
20 ÷ 2 =	30 ÷ 3 =	50 ÷ 5 =	11 ÷ 1 =	40 ÷ 4 =
36 ÷ 6 =	35 ÷ 7 =	32 ÷ 8 =	20 ÷ 10 =	1 ÷ 1 =
14 ÷ 7 =	70 ÷ 7 =	88 ÷ 8 =	70 ÷ 10 =	36 ÷ 12 =
14 ÷ 2 =	12 ÷ 12 =	66 ÷ 6 =	108 ÷ 12 =	24 ÷ 2 =
42 ÷ 7 =	15 ÷ 3 =	60 ÷ 10 =	120 ÷ 12 =	72 ÷ 8 =
0 ÷ 6 =	2 ÷ 2 =	33 ÷ 11 =	77 ÷ 11 =	72 ÷ 12 =

7 ÷ 7 =	9 ÷ 9 =	12 ÷ 2 =	90 ÷ 9 =	12 ÷ 6 =
25 ÷ 5 =	22 ÷ 2 =	99 ÷ 11 =	0 ÷ 9 =	20 ÷ 10 =
1 ÷ 1 =	56 ÷ 8 =	30 ÷ 3 =	6 ÷ 6 =	20 ÷ 2 =
48 ÷ 6 =	72 ÷ 6 =	84 ÷ 12 =	63 ÷ 7 =	6 ÷ 3 =
36 ÷ 12 =	60 ÷ 6 =	80 ÷ 10 =	120 ÷ 10 =	0 ÷ 3 =
63 ÷ 9 =	60 ÷ 5 =	0 ÷ 4 =	16 ÷ 4 =	90 ÷ 10 =
3 ÷ 3 =	24 ÷ 2 =	32 ÷ 8 =	56 ÷ 7 =	30 ÷ 10 =
24 ÷ 6 =	18 ÷ 9 =	64 ÷ 8 =	10 ÷ 10 =	96 ÷ 8 =
48 ÷ 12 =	88 ÷ 11 =	10 ÷ 5 =	50 ÷ 5 =	30 ÷ 6 =
49 ÷ 7 =	7 ÷ 1 =	42 ÷ 7 =	77 ÷ 7 =	36 ÷ 6 =
99 ÷ 9 =	18 ÷ 6 =	15 ÷ 3 =	24 ÷ 3 =	48 ÷ 4 =
0 ÷ 8 =	0 ÷ 7 =	55 ÷ 11 =	100 ÷ 10 =	14 ÷ 2 =
35 ÷ 5 =	12 ÷ 4 =	11 ÷ 11 =	12 ÷ 3 =	20 ÷ 4 =
72 ÷ 12 =	2 ÷ 1 =	10 ÷ 1 =	27 ÷ 3 =	33 ÷ 3 =
24 ÷ 12 =	80 ÷ 8 =	9 ÷ 1 =	28 ÷ 7 =	50 ÷ 10 =
4 ÷ 2 =	72 ÷ 8 =	60 ÷ 10 =	3 ÷ 1 =	16 ÷ 2 =
18 ÷ 2 =	0 ÷ 5 =	16 ÷ 8 =	36 ÷ 9 =	108 ÷ 12 =
121 ÷ 11 =	20 ÷ 5 =	88 ÷ 8 =	14 ÷ 7 =	30 ÷ 5 =
4 ÷ 1 =	66 ÷ 11 =	24 ÷ 4 =	96 ÷ 12 =	15 ÷ 5 =
33 ÷ 11 =	12 ÷ 1 =	5 ÷ 1 =	77 ÷ 11 =	8 ÷ 2 =

Name _____   Date _____

0 ÷ 3 =	70 ÷ 7 =	10 ÷ 2 =	0 ÷ 2 =	110 ÷ 11 =
12 ÷ 2 =	36 ÷ 9 =	10 ÷ 5 =	10 ÷ 1 =	120 ÷ 10 =
72 ÷ 6 =	48 ÷ 6 =	81 ÷ 9 =	55 ÷ 11 =	12 ÷ 12 =
21 ÷ 3 =	3 ÷ 1 =	88 ÷ 11 =	50 ÷ 5 =	3 ÷ 3 =
40 ÷ 8 =	30 ÷ 5 =	55 ÷ 5 =	54 ÷ 9 =	6 ÷ 2 =
48 ÷ 8 =	10 ÷ 10 =	48 ÷ 12 =	84 ÷ 7 =	90 ÷ 9 =
132 ÷ 12 =	11 ÷ 11 =	12 ÷ 3 =	60 ÷ 5 =	24 ÷ 2 =
77 ÷ 11 =	60 ÷ 12 =	49 ÷ 7 =	4 ÷ 2 =	30 ÷ 10 =
72 ÷ 9 =	27 ÷ 3 =	36 ÷ 4 =	28 ÷ 7 =	20 ÷ 4 =
6 ÷ 6 =	20 ÷ 5 =	36 ÷ 6 =	0 ÷ 11 =	22 ÷ 2 =
99 ÷ 9 =	56 ÷ 7 =	8 ÷ 4 =	4 ÷ 1 =	6 ÷ 3 =
7 ÷ 7 =	108 ÷ 9 =	70 ÷ 10 =	14 ÷ 2 =	33 ÷ 3 =
30 ÷ 3 =	32 ÷ 4 =	42 ÷ 7 =	8 ÷ 2 =	60 ÷ 10 =
56 ÷ 8 =	21 ÷ 7 =	120 ÷ 12 =	45 ÷ 9 =	2 ÷ 2 =
99 ÷ 11 =	0 ÷ 1 =	24 ÷ 3 =	80 ÷ 10 =	16 ÷ 4 =
100 ÷ 10 =	22 ÷ 11 =	42 ÷ 6 =	36 ÷ 12 =	18 ÷ 9 =
12 ÷ 1 =	35 ÷ 7 =	15 ÷ 5 =	121 ÷ 11 =	72 ÷ 8 =
44 ÷ 11 =	108 ÷ 12 =	0 ÷ 12 =	66 ÷ 11 =	4 ÷ 4 =
32 ÷ 8 =	72 ÷ 12 =	45 ÷ 5 =	8 ÷ 8 =	35 ÷ 5 =
40 ÷ 5 =	9 ÷ 1 =	0 ÷ 6 =	60 ÷ 6 =	24 ÷ 6 =

Name _____   Date _____

8 ÷ 8 =	5 ÷ 5 =	36 ÷ 3 =	10 ÷ 1 =	40 ÷ 5 =
50 ÷ 5 =	132 ÷ 11 =	20 ÷ 5 =	15 ÷ 5 =	21 ÷ 3 =
2 ÷ 1 =	24 ÷ 4 =	30 ÷ 6 =	28 ÷ 7 =	8 ÷ 4 =
40 ÷ 10 =	21 ÷ 7 =	6 ÷ 2 =	96 ÷ 12 =	3 ÷ 3 =
81 ÷ 9 =	0 ÷ 7 =	4 ÷ 2 =	121 ÷ 11 =	36 ÷ 12 =
36 ÷ 4 =	4 ÷ 1 =	7 ÷ 7 =	12 ÷ 2 =	77 ÷ 11 =
24 ÷ 3 =	14 ÷ 7 =	2 ÷ 2 =	120 ÷ 12 =	0 ÷ 4 =
63 ÷ 9 =	88 ÷ 11 =	9 ÷ 3 =	72 ÷ 9 =	48 ÷ 4 =
48 ÷ 6 =	20 ÷ 10 =	99 ÷ 9 =	5 ÷ 1 =	0 ÷ 3 =
24 ÷ 12 =	7 ÷ 1 =	12 ÷ 3 =	44 ÷ 11 =	0 ÷ 11 =
54 ÷ 6 =	56 ÷ 7 =	84 ÷ 7 =	6 ÷ 6 =	3 ÷ 1 =
42 ÷ 6 =	70 ÷ 10 =	36 ÷ 6 =	11 ÷ 11 =	12 ÷ 4 =
33 ÷ 3 =	0 ÷ 2 =	30 ÷ 10 =	54 ÷ 9 =	11 ÷ 1 =
60 ÷ 12 =	20 ÷ 4 =	8 ÷ 1 =	27 ÷ 3 =	0 ÷ 9 =
120 ÷ 10 =	42 ÷ 7 =	15 ÷ 3 =	12 ÷ 1 =	18 ÷ 2 =
14 ÷ 2 =	16 ÷ 4 =	12 ÷ 6 =	108 ÷ 12 =	6 ÷ 1 =
80 ÷ 10 =	18 ÷ 6 =	40 ÷ 4 =	55 ÷ 11 =	63 ÷ 7 =
55 ÷ 5 =	132 ÷ 12 =	48 ÷ 8 =	9 ÷ 9 =	0 ÷ 6 =
60 ÷ 5 =	77 ÷ 7 =	110 ÷ 11 =	24 ÷ 2 =	10 ÷ 10 =
12 ÷ 12 =	9 ÷ 1 =	27 ÷ 9 =	30 ÷ 3 =	35 ÷ 5 =

Name _____   Date _____

0 ÷ 3 =	0 ÷ 2 =	0 ÷ 9 =	40 ÷ 8 =	8 ÷ 8 =
48 ÷ 8 =	72 ÷ 12 =	5 ÷ 1 =	12 ÷ 3 =	40 ÷ 10 =
2 ÷ 1 =	0 ÷ 11 =	49 ÷ 7 =	36 ÷ 6 =	48 ÷ 6 =
10 ÷ 5 =	8 ÷ 4 =	90 ÷ 9 =	50 ÷ 10 =	27 ÷ 9 =
24 ÷ 12 =	20 ÷ 4 =	42 ÷ 7 =	120 ÷ 12 =	35 ÷ 7 =
22 ÷ 11 =	6 ÷ 3 =	88 ÷ 8 =	36 ÷ 4 =	55 ÷ 11 =
60 ÷ 12 =	7 ÷ 7 =	11 ÷ 1 =	4 ÷ 4 =	0 ÷ 5 =
0 ÷ 12 =	28 ÷ 4 =	48 ÷ 12 =	99 ÷ 9 =	80 ÷ 10 =
33 ÷ 3 =	84 ÷ 7 =	7 ÷ 1 =	15 ÷ 3 =	20 ÷ 5 =
30 ÷ 10 =	3 ÷ 1 =	84 ÷ 12 =	45 ÷ 5 =	96 ÷ 8 =
60 ÷ 5 =	0 ÷ 8 =	0 ÷ 6 =	2 ÷ 2 =	6 ÷ 1 =
18 ÷ 3 =	63 ÷ 9 =	64 ÷ 8 =	45 ÷ 9 =	15 ÷ 5 =
5 ÷ 5 =	44 ÷ 4 =	27 ÷ 3 =	10 ÷ 10 =	1 ÷ 1 =
108 ÷ 12 =	10 ÷ 2 =	88 ÷ 11 =	99 ÷ 11 =	18 ÷ 9 =
60 ÷ 10 =	32 ÷ 8 =	24 ÷ 2 =	8 ÷ 2 =	18 ÷ 6 =
40 ÷ 5 =	4 ÷ 2 =	54 ÷ 9 =	90 ÷ 10 =	9 ÷ 1 =
3 ÷ 3 =	70 ÷ 10 =	9 ÷ 3 =	35 ÷ 5 =	16 ÷ 2 =
55 ÷ 5 =	16 ÷ 4 =	72 ÷ 9 =	96 ÷ 12 =	4 ÷ 1 =
60 ÷ 6 =	121 ÷ 11 =	9 ÷ 9 =	16 ÷ 8 =	42 ÷ 6 =
36 ÷ 12 =	56 ÷ 8 =	63 ÷ 7 =	12 ÷ 4 =	11 ÷ 11 =

40 ÷ 8 =	0 ÷ 9 =	4 ÷ 4 =	12 ÷ 3 =	7 ÷ 7 =
55 ÷ 11 =	24 ÷ 6 =	24 ÷ 8 =	70 ÷ 7 =	56 ÷ 8 =
0 ÷ 8 =	24 ÷ 4 =	12 ÷ 4 =	1 ÷ 1 =	12 ÷ 12 =
30 ÷ 3 =	5 ÷ 1 =	72 ÷ 9 =	110 ÷ 11 =	99 ÷ 11 =
14 ÷ 2 =	42 ÷ 7 =	44 ÷ 11 =	24 ÷ 3 =	4 ÷ 2 =
36 ÷ 9 =	12 ÷ 2 =	12 ÷ 1 =	99 ÷ 9 =	32 ÷ 4 =
8 ÷ 2 =	132 ÷ 12 =	27 ÷ 3 =	80 ÷ 8 =	21 ÷ 7 =
100 ÷ 10 =	6 ÷ 1 =	60 ÷ 6 =	10 ÷ 2 =	54 ÷ 9 =
45 ÷ 5 =	55 ÷ 5 =	63 ÷ 7 =	27 ÷ 9 =	0 ÷ 10 =
10 ÷ 10 =	20 ÷ 2 =	3 ÷ 1 =	45 ÷ 9 =	48 ÷ 6 =
0 ÷ 7 =	0 ÷ 1 =	5 ÷ 5 =	4 ÷ 1 =	7 ÷ 1 =
20 ÷ 10 =	18 ÷ 6 =	70 ÷ 10 =	21 ÷ 3 =	60 ÷ 10 =
64 ÷ 8 =	3 ÷ 3 =	54 ÷ 6 =	108 ÷ 9 =	15 ÷ 5 =
36 ÷ 6 =	48 ÷ 8 =	48 ÷ 12 =	90 ÷ 10 =	84 ÷ 7 =
6 ÷ 6 =	81 ÷ 9 =	22 ÷ 2 =	28 ÷ 7 =	14 ÷ 7 =
50 ÷ 10 =	77 ÷ 11 =	49 ÷ 7 =	0 ÷ 4 =	40 ÷ 5 =
35 ÷ 5 =	8 ÷ 1 =	36 ÷ 12 =	18 ÷ 9 =	77 ÷ 7 =
6 ÷ 2 =	0 ÷ 6 =	16 ÷ 4 =	18 ÷ 3 =	9 ÷ 3 =
44 ÷ 4 =	42 ÷ 6 =	0 ÷ 11 =	20 ÷ 4 =	0 ÷ 5 =
63 ÷ 9 =	10 ÷ 1 =	36 ÷ 4 =	40 ÷ 10 =	72 ÷ 8 =

Name _____ Date _____

40 ÷ 5 =	84 ÷ 12 =	44 ÷ 4 =	12 ÷ 3 =	27 ÷ 3 =
36 ÷ 12 =	20 ÷ 4 =	99 ÷ 11 =	27 ÷ 9 =	72 ÷ 6 =
96 ÷ 12 =	66 ÷ 6 =	36 ÷ 3 =	50 ÷ 5 =	25 ÷ 5 =
121 ÷ 11 =	35 ÷ 5 =	80 ÷ 10 =	36 ÷ 9 =	33 ÷ 11 =
35 ÷ 7 =	84 ÷ 7 =	48 ÷ 12 =	54 ÷ 9 =	99 ÷ 9 =
21 ÷ 3 =	72 ÷ 9 =	72 ÷ 12 =	15 ÷ 5 =	63 ÷ 7 =
108 ÷ 9 =	55 ÷ 11 =	48 ÷ 4 =	24 ÷ 6 =	110 ÷ 11 =
33 ÷ 3 =	70 ÷ 10 =	132 ÷ 11 =	81 ÷ 9 =	30 ÷ 10 =
21 ÷ 7 =	77 ÷ 11 =	64 ÷ 8 =	32 ÷ 4 =	88 ÷ 8 =
28 ÷ 4 =	32 ÷ 8 =	72 ÷ 8 =	16 ÷ 4 =	48 ÷ 6 =
60 ÷ 5 =	77 ÷ 7 =	108 ÷ 12 =	110 ÷ 10 =	24 ÷ 3 =
9 ÷ 3 =	54 ÷ 6 =	30 ÷ 5 =	120 ÷ 10 =	40 ÷ 10 =
90 ÷ 10 =	60 ÷ 12 =	40 ÷ 4 =	66 ÷ 11 =	48 ÷ 8 =
12 ÷ 4 =	50 ÷ 10 =	30 ÷ 6 =	24 ÷ 4 =	30 ÷ 3 =
120 ÷ 12 =	56 ÷ 7 =	96 ÷ 8 =	56 ÷ 8 =	18 ÷ 3 =
28 ÷ 7 =	132 ÷ 12 =	90 ÷ 9 =	44 ÷ 11 =	60 ÷ 6 =
70 ÷ 7 =	24 ÷ 8 =	18 ÷ 6 =	42 ÷ 6 =	144 ÷ 12 =
42 ÷ 7 =	45 ÷ 9 =	80 ÷ 8 =	40 ÷ 8 =	60 ÷ 10 =
36 ÷ 6 =	20 ÷ 5 =	88 ÷ 11 =	63 ÷ 9 =	15 ÷ 3 =
36 ÷ 4 =	100 ÷ 10 =	55 ÷ 5 =	49 ÷ 7 =	45 ÷ 5 =

56 ÷ 8 =	72 ÷ 12 =	40 ÷ 10 =	44 ÷ 11 =	84 ÷ 12 =
99 ÷ 9 =	21 ÷ 3 =	90 ÷ 9 =	28 ÷ 4 =	60 ÷ 6 =
40 ÷ 5 =	35 ÷ 5 =	63 ÷ 7 =	36 ÷ 9 =	132 ÷ 12 =
60 ÷ 12 =	88 ÷ 11 =	30 ÷ 10 =	90 ÷ 10 =	108 ÷ 9 =
27 ÷ 3 =	56 ÷ 7 =	44 ÷ 4 =	120 ÷ 10 =	70 ÷ 7 =
55 ÷ 5 =	42 ÷ 7 =	49 ÷ 7 =	54 ÷ 9 =	110 ÷ 10 =
48 ÷ 12 =	28 ÷ 7 =	24 ÷ 8 =	77 ÷ 7 =	120 ÷ 12 =
63 ÷ 9 =	27 ÷ 9 =	25 ÷ 5 =	48 ÷ 8 =	21 ÷ 7 =
12 ÷ 3 =	24 ÷ 6 =	16 ÷ 4 =	144 ÷ 12 =	72 ÷ 8 =
48 ÷ 6 =	54 ÷ 6 =	36 ÷ 6 =	32 ÷ 8 =	72 ÷ 9 =
42 ÷ 6 =	20 ÷ 5 =	132 ÷ 11 =	45 ÷ 9 =	72 ÷ 6 =
99 ÷ 11 =	33 ÷ 3 =	96 ÷ 12 =	36 ÷ 4 =	96 ÷ 8 =
12 ÷ 4 =	33 ÷ 11 =	9 ÷ 3 =	15 ÷ 3 =	45 ÷ 5 =
60 ÷ 10 =	88 ÷ 8 =	30 ÷ 6 =	110 ÷ 11 =	50 ÷ 5 =
24 ÷ 3 =	80 ÷ 8 =	15 ÷ 5 =	60 ÷ 5 =	40 ÷ 4 =
121 ÷ 11 =	108 ÷ 12 =	24 ÷ 4 =	50 ÷ 10 =	66 ÷ 6 =
66 ÷ 11 =	18 ÷ 6 =	64 ÷ 8 =	36 ÷ 12 =	36 ÷ 3 =
48 ÷ 4 =	18 ÷ 3 =	55 ÷ 11 =	81 ÷ 9 =	30 ÷ 5 =
77 ÷ 11 =	80 ÷ 10 =	35 ÷ 7 =	20 ÷ 4 =	32 ÷ 4 =
30 ÷ 3 =	70 ÷ 10 =	84 ÷ 7 =	40 ÷ 8 =	100 ÷ 10 =

Name _____ Date _____

40 ÷ 10 =	42 ÷ 6 =	20 ÷ 5 =	48 ÷ 8 =	50 ÷ 5 =
12 ÷ 4 =	90 ÷ 9 =	50 ÷ 10 =	120 ÷ 10 =	45 ÷ 5 =
66 ÷ 11 =	72 ÷ 12 =	30 ÷ 5 =	45 ÷ 9 =	144 ÷ 12 =
132 ÷ 11 =	80 ÷ 10 =	60 ÷ 10 =	80 ÷ 8 =	30 ÷ 6 =
36 ÷ 3 =	20 ÷ 4 =	110 ÷ 10 =	56 ÷ 7 =	36 ÷ 6 =
84 ÷ 12 =	18 ÷ 3 =	40 ÷ 5 =	21 ÷ 3 =	66 ÷ 6 =
18 ÷ 6 =	12 ÷ 3 =	15 ÷ 5 =	24 ÷ 6 =	77 ÷ 7 =
99 ÷ 9 =	28 ÷ 4 =	54 ÷ 9 =	55 ÷ 11 =	60 ÷ 6 =
48 ÷ 6 =	63 ÷ 9 =	96 ÷ 12 =	99 ÷ 11 =	96 ÷ 8 =
72 ÷ 6 =	30 ÷ 3 =	33 ÷ 3 =	32 ÷ 4 =	40 ÷ 8 =
110 ÷ 11 =	88 ÷ 8 =	40 ÷ 4 =	42 ÷ 7 =	70 ÷ 10 =
24 ÷ 4 =	24 ÷ 8 =	56 ÷ 8 =	9 ÷ 3 =	48 ÷ 4 =
84 ÷ 7 =	60 ÷ 12 =	70 ÷ 7 =	108 ÷ 12 =	21 ÷ 7 =
48 ÷ 12 =	36 ÷ 9 =	27 ÷ 9 =	35 ÷ 7 =	44 ÷ 11 =
44 ÷ 4 =	55 ÷ 5 =	33 ÷ 11 =	30 ÷ 10 =	15 ÷ 3 =
49 ÷ 7 =	100 ÷ 10 =	32 ÷ 8 =	81 ÷ 9 =	108 ÷ 9 =
24 ÷ 3 =	28 ÷ 7 =	25 ÷ 5 =	16 ÷ 4 =	36 ÷ 12 =
27 ÷ 3 =	72 ÷ 9 =	36 ÷ 4 =	60 ÷ 5 =	54 ÷ 6 =
35 ÷ 5 =	120 ÷ 12 =	88 ÷ 11 =	63 ÷ 7 =	64 ÷ 8 =
72 ÷ 8 =	132 ÷ 12 =	121 ÷ 11 =	77 ÷ 11 =	90 ÷ 10 =

25 ÷ 5 =	84 ÷ 12 =	35 ÷ 7 =	40 ÷ 10 =	36 ÷ 6 =
99 ÷ 9 =	27 ÷ 3 =	60 ÷ 6 =	121 ÷ 11 =	110 ÷ 11 =
132 ÷ 12 =	35 ÷ 5 =	44 ÷ 11 =	55 ÷ 5 =	77 ÷ 11 =
40 ÷ 5 =	36 ÷ 9 =	24 ÷ 3 =	21 ÷ 3 =	54 ÷ 6 =
28 ÷ 7 =	88 ÷ 8 =	50 ÷ 5 =	18 ÷ 3 =	108 ÷ 12 =
50 ÷ 10 =	32 ÷ 8 =	100 ÷ 10 =	99 ÷ 11 =	30 ÷ 5 =
45 ÷ 9 =	55 ÷ 11 =	28 ÷ 4 =	24 ÷ 4 =	36 ÷ 3 =
72 ÷ 12 =	108 ÷ 9 =	77 ÷ 7 =	40 ÷ 4 =	9 ÷ 3 =
64 ÷ 8 =	42 ÷ 6 =	45 ÷ 5 =	12 ÷ 4 =	33 ÷ 11 =
12 ÷ 3 =	70 ÷ 7 =	36 ÷ 12 =	30 ÷ 10 =	27 ÷ 9 =
66 ÷ 11 =	80 ÷ 10 =	60 ÷ 10 =	15 ÷ 5 =	54 ÷ 9 =
48 ÷ 8 =	96 ÷ 8 =	16 ÷ 4 =	132 ÷ 11 =	44 ÷ 4 =
80 ÷ 8 =	48 ÷ 12 =	18 ÷ 6 =	30 ÷ 3 =	66 ÷ 6 =
90 ÷ 9 =	48 ÷ 4 =	49 ÷ 7 =	48 ÷ 6 =	24 ÷ 8 =
24 ÷ 6 =	36 ÷ 4 =	72 ÷ 6 =	88 ÷ 11 =	21 ÷ 7 =
42 ÷ 7 =	81 ÷ 9 =	84 ÷ 7 =	72 ÷ 9 =	110 ÷ 10 =
20 ÷ 5 =	120 ÷ 12 =	56 ÷ 8 =	15 ÷ 3 =	30 ÷ 6 =
120 ÷ 10 =	96 ÷ 12 =	32 ÷ 4 =	72 ÷ 8 =	56 ÷ 7 =
90 ÷ 10 =	60 ÷ 5 =	63 ÷ 7 =	20 ÷ 4 =	144 ÷ 12 =
63 ÷ 9 =	70 ÷ 10 =	33 ÷ 3 =	60 ÷ 12 =	40 ÷ 8 =

Name _____   Date _____

$30 \div 6 =$	$15 \div 3 =$	$63 \div 7 =$	$24 \div 4 =$	$28 \div 7 =$
$96 \div 12 =$	$54 \div 6 =$	$30 \div 5 =$	$120 \div 12 =$	$70 \div 7 =$
$28 \div 4 =$	$24 \div 8 =$	$70 \div 10 =$	$36 \div 6 =$	$9 \div 3 =$
$32 \div 4 =$	$90 \div 9 =$	$35 \div 7 =$	$121 \div 11 =$	$66 \div 11 =$
$35 \div 5 =$	$80 \div 8 =$	$48 \div 4 =$	$50 \div 5 =$	$24 \div 3 =$
$54 \div 9 =$	$72 \div 12 =$	$21 \div 7 =$	$120 \div 10 =$	$45 \div 9 =$
$110 \div 11 =$	$99 \div 11 =$	$48 \div 8 =$	$72 \div 9 =$	$132 \div 11 =$
$20 \div 4 =$	$25 \div 5 =$	$56 \div 8 =$	$77 \div 7 =$	$144 \div 12 =$
$100 \div 10 =$	$49 \div 7 =$	$36 \div 12 =$	$60 \div 5 =$	$15 \div 5 =$
$30 \div 3 =$	$96 \div 8 =$	$24 \div 6 =$	$88 \div 11 =$	$72 \div 6 =$
$27 \div 9 =$	$42 \div 6 =$	$80 \div 10 =$	$84 \div 12 =$	$56 \div 7 =$
$36 \div 3 =$	$44 \div 4 =$	$63 \div 9 =$	$55 \div 5 =$	$44 \div 11 =$
$110 \div 10 =$	$18 \div 6 =$	$42 \div 7 =$	$88 \div 8 =$	$36 \div 9 =$
$30 \div 10 =$	$108 \div 9 =$	$60 \div 6 =$	$48 \div 12 =$	$12 \div 3 =$
$33 \div 11 =$	$18 \div 3 =$	$108 \div 12 =$	$32 \div 8 =$	$64 \div 8 =$
$99 \div 9 =$	$12 \div 4 =$	$60 \div 10 =$	$60 \div 12 =$	$66 \div 6 =$
$45 \div 5 =$	$72 \div 8 =$	$27 \div 3 =$	$90 \div 10 =$	$48 \div 6 =$
$33 \div 3 =$	$20 \div 5 =$	$77 \div 11 =$	$81 \div 9 =$	$40 \div 5 =$
$16 \div 4 =$	$36 \div 4 =$	$55 \div 11 =$	$21 \div 3 =$	$40 \div 8 =$
$40 \div 4 =$	$40 \div 10 =$	$132 \div 12 =$	$84 \div 7 =$	$50 \div 10 =$

28 ÷ 4 =	108 ÷ 9 =	132 ÷ 12 =	25 ÷ 5 =	40 ÷ 10 =
110 ÷ 10 =	96 ÷ 12 =	55 ÷ 5 =	120 ÷ 12 =	35 ÷ 7 =
132 ÷ 11 =	20 ÷ 4 =	77 ÷ 11 =	28 ÷ 7 =	50 ÷ 5 =
15 ÷ 5 =	24 ÷ 6 =	16 ÷ 4 =	64 ÷ 8 =	44 ÷ 4 =
88 ÷ 8 =	45 ÷ 9 =	121 ÷ 11 =	60 ÷ 6 =	27 ÷ 9 =
63 ÷ 9 =	27 ÷ 3 =	33 ÷ 3 =	12 ÷ 3 =	77 ÷ 7 =
30 ÷ 3 =	84 ÷ 12 =	15 ÷ 3 =	21 ÷ 7 =	100 ÷ 10 =
36 ÷ 12 =	72 ÷ 12 =	36 ÷ 6 =	42 ÷ 7 =	30 ÷ 10 =
54 ÷ 9 =	80 ÷ 8 =	90 ÷ 9 =	30 ÷ 6 =	48 ÷ 4 =
30 ÷ 5 =	56 ÷ 8 =	110 ÷ 11 =	18 ÷ 6 =	72 ÷ 6 =
32 ÷ 8 =	24 ÷ 4 =	81 ÷ 9 =	96 ÷ 8 =	48 ÷ 6 =
70 ÷ 7 =	49 ÷ 7 =	12 ÷ 4 =	40 ÷ 4 =	108 ÷ 12 =
63 ÷ 7 =	99 ÷ 11 =	70 ÷ 10 =	80 ÷ 10 =	18 ÷ 3 =
48 ÷ 12 =	54 ÷ 6 =	66 ÷ 11 =	36 ÷ 9 =	60 ÷ 12 =
20 ÷ 5 =	99 ÷ 9 =	44 ÷ 11 =	48 ÷ 8 =	88 ÷ 11 =
72 ÷ 9 =	90 ÷ 10 =	21 ÷ 3 =	72 ÷ 8 =	60 ÷ 5 =
56 ÷ 7 =	66 ÷ 6 =	9 ÷ 3 =	33 ÷ 11 =	55 ÷ 11 =
36 ÷ 3 =	45 ÷ 5 =	60 ÷ 10 =	144 ÷ 12 =	40 ÷ 8 =
120 ÷ 10 =	42 ÷ 6 =	35 ÷ 5 =	36 ÷ 4 =	40 ÷ 5 =
32 ÷ 4 =	50 ÷ 10 =	24 ÷ 8 =	84 ÷ 7 =	24 ÷ 3 =

Name _____   Date _____

96 ÷ 8 =	21 ÷ 7 =	108 ÷ 12 =	56 ÷ 8 =	30 ÷ 6 =
72 ÷ 8 =	24 ÷ 6 =	36 ÷ 12 =	48 ÷ 8 =	40 ÷ 4 =
96 ÷ 12 =	42 ÷ 6 =	72 ÷ 12 =	66 ÷ 11 =	30 ÷ 10 =
20 ÷ 4 =	80 ÷ 10 =	132 ÷ 12 =	48 ÷ 4 =	40 ÷ 10 =
9 ÷ 3 =	64 ÷ 8 =	27 ÷ 3 =	48 ÷ 12 =	15 ÷ 5 =
12 ÷ 3 =	60 ÷ 10 =	44 ÷ 11 =	48 ÷ 6 =	80 ÷ 8 =
27 ÷ 9 =	20 ÷ 5 =	28 ÷ 4 =	24 ÷ 4 =	99 ÷ 9 =
50 ÷ 5 =	56 ÷ 7 =	30 ÷ 3 =	28 ÷ 7 =	121 ÷ 11 =
25 ÷ 5 =	120 ÷ 10 =	110 ÷ 11 =	36 ÷ 4 =	81 ÷ 9 =
36 ÷ 9 =	35 ÷ 5 =	77 ÷ 7 =	35 ÷ 7 =	40 ÷ 5 =
66 ÷ 6 =	70 ÷ 7 =	50 ÷ 10 =	16 ÷ 4 =	90 ÷ 10 =
72 ÷ 6 =	90 ÷ 9 =	144 ÷ 12 =	44 ÷ 4 =	84 ÷ 12 =
15 ÷ 3 =	120 ÷ 12 =	108 ÷ 9 =	88 ÷ 11 =	110 ÷ 10 =
55 ÷ 11 =	60 ÷ 5 =	18 ÷ 6 =	60 ÷ 6 =	45 ÷ 5 =
30 ÷ 5 =	40 ÷ 8 =	24 ÷ 8 =	70 ÷ 10 =	12 ÷ 4 =
100 ÷ 10 =	32 ÷ 8 =	32 ÷ 4 =	88 ÷ 8 =	21 ÷ 3 =
77 ÷ 11 =	60 ÷ 12 =	45 ÷ 9 =	54 ÷ 6 =	63 ÷ 7 =
42 ÷ 7 =	18 ÷ 3 =	55 ÷ 5 =	24 ÷ 3 =	49 ÷ 7 =
33 ÷ 11 =	54 ÷ 9 =	36 ÷ 6 =	84 ÷ 7 =	33 ÷ 3 =
132 ÷ 11 =	72 ÷ 9 =	36 ÷ 3 =	99 ÷ 11 =	63 ÷ 9 =

Name _____   Date _____

18 ÷ 6 =	120 ÷ 12 =	66 ÷ 11 =	20 ÷ 5 =	40 ÷ 4 =
12 ÷ 4 =	60 ÷ 5 =	48 ÷ 4 =	63 ÷ 9 =	132 ÷ 12 =
88 ÷ 11 =	84 ÷ 12 =	80 ÷ 10 =	81 ÷ 9 =	55 ÷ 11 =
110 ÷ 10 =	70 ÷ 7 =	66 ÷ 6 =	30 ÷ 3 =	36 ÷ 12 =
54 ÷ 6 =	96 ÷ 8 =	42 ÷ 7 =	56 ÷ 8 =	20 ÷ 4 =
49 ÷ 7 =	56 ÷ 7 =	72 ÷ 12 =	120 ÷ 10 =	40 ÷ 8 =
30 ÷ 5 =	9 ÷ 3 =	54 ÷ 9 =	48 ÷ 6 =	50 ÷ 10 =
110 ÷ 11 =	80 ÷ 8 =	40 ÷ 5 =	28 ÷ 7 =	24 ÷ 6 =
60 ÷ 6 =	48 ÷ 8 =	77 ÷ 11 =	36 ÷ 4 =	24 ÷ 4 =
42 ÷ 6 =	60 ÷ 12 =	28 ÷ 4 =	99 ÷ 9 =	45 ÷ 9 =
36 ÷ 9 =	72 ÷ 9 =	44 ÷ 11 =	77 ÷ 7 =	84 ÷ 7 =
36 ÷ 3 =	90 ÷ 9 =	15 ÷ 5 =	108 ÷ 9 =	21 ÷ 3 =
72 ÷ 8 =	99 ÷ 11 =	90 ÷ 10 =	12 ÷ 3 =	108 ÷ 12 =
15 ÷ 3 =	100 ÷ 10 =	35 ÷ 7 =	33 ÷ 11 =	132 ÷ 11 =
32 ÷ 8 =	48 ÷ 12 =	44 ÷ 4 =	64 ÷ 8 =	16 ÷ 4 =
30 ÷ 6 =	40 ÷ 10 =	144 ÷ 12 =	121 ÷ 11 =	21 ÷ 7 =
70 ÷ 10 =	24 ÷ 3 =	96 ÷ 12 =	60 ÷ 10 =	88 ÷ 8 =
27 ÷ 3 =	50 ÷ 5 =	45 ÷ 5 =	55 ÷ 5 =	63 ÷ 7 =
25 ÷ 5 =	18 ÷ 3 =	30 ÷ 10 =	36 ÷ 6 =	24 ÷ 8 =
35 ÷ 5 =	27 ÷ 9 =	72 ÷ 6 =	33 ÷ 3 =	32 ÷ 4 =

Name _____   Date _____

80 ÷ 8 =	18 ÷ 6 =	36 ÷ 9 =	66 ÷ 11 =	56 ÷ 8 =
24 ÷ 8 =	80 ÷ 10 =	15 ÷ 5 =	15 ÷ 3 =	16 ÷ 4 =
72 ÷ 9 =	20 ÷ 4 =	44 ÷ 4 =	96 ÷ 8 =	55 ÷ 5 =
72 ÷ 6 =	108 ÷ 12 =	54 ÷ 6 =	12 ÷ 3 =	21 ÷ 7 =
48 ÷ 12 =	35 ÷ 5 =	48 ÷ 6 =	28 ÷ 4 =	27 ÷ 9 =
20 ÷ 5 =	50 ÷ 10 =	27 ÷ 3 =	33 ÷ 11 =	54 ÷ 9 =
50 ÷ 5 =	44 ÷ 11 =	60 ÷ 5 =	24 ÷ 4 =	36 ÷ 4 =
35 ÷ 7 =	30 ÷ 3 =	40 ÷ 10 =	132 ÷ 11 =	110 ÷ 10 =
32 ÷ 8 =	100 ÷ 10 =	60 ÷ 10 =	24 ÷ 3 =	120 ÷ 12 =
70 ÷ 7 =	99 ÷ 11 =	72 ÷ 8 =	30 ÷ 5 =	84 ÷ 12 =
36 ÷ 12 =	32 ÷ 4 =	99 ÷ 9 =	36 ÷ 3 =	121 ÷ 11 =
72 ÷ 12 =	48 ÷ 8 =	90 ÷ 9 =	110 ÷ 11 =	96 ÷ 12 =
70 ÷ 10 =	77 ÷ 7 =	55 ÷ 11 =	64 ÷ 8 =	45 ÷ 9 =
9 ÷ 3 =	90 ÷ 10 =	40 ÷ 5 =	40 ÷ 8 =	132 ÷ 12 =
60 ÷ 6 =	36 ÷ 6 =	24 ÷ 6 =	60 ÷ 12 =	40 ÷ 4 =
49 ÷ 7 =	77 ÷ 11 =	63 ÷ 7 =	25 ÷ 5 =	88 ÷ 11 =
56 ÷ 7 =	63 ÷ 9 =	120 ÷ 10 =	28 ÷ 7 =	33 ÷ 3 =
88 ÷ 8 =	48 ÷ 4 =	42 ÷ 6 =	108 ÷ 9 =	30 ÷ 6 =
144 ÷ 12 =	12 ÷ 4 =	66 ÷ 6 =	21 ÷ 3 =	81 ÷ 9 =
45 ÷ 5 =	42 ÷ 7 =	18 ÷ 3 =	30 ÷ 10 =	84 ÷ 7 =

Name _____ Date _____

36 ÷ 6 =	77 ÷ 11 =	45 ÷ 5 =	84 ÷ 12 =	60 ÷ 5 =
88 ÷ 11 =	15 ÷ 5 =	44 ÷ 11 =	42 ÷ 6 =	33 ÷ 3 =
32 ÷ 4 =	77 ÷ 7 =	30 ÷ 3 =	49 ÷ 7 =	110 ÷ 11 =
72 ÷ 9 =	15 ÷ 3 =	21 ÷ 3 =	64 ÷ 8 =	50 ÷ 5 =
35 ÷ 7 =	72 ÷ 12 =	28 ÷ 7 =	30 ÷ 5 =	30 ÷ 10 =
32 ÷ 8 =	36 ÷ 9 =	54 ÷ 6 =	108 ÷ 12 =	24 ÷ 8 =
20 ÷ 4 =	27 ÷ 3 =	63 ÷ 9 =	50 ÷ 10 =	12 ÷ 3 =
63 ÷ 7 =	80 ÷ 10 =	120 ÷ 12 =	56 ÷ 7 =	42 ÷ 7 =
99 ÷ 9 =	70 ÷ 10 =	90 ÷ 10 =	35 ÷ 5 =	81 ÷ 9 =
96 ÷ 12 =	48 ÷ 4 =	55 ÷ 5 =	16 ÷ 4 =	40 ÷ 5 =
110 ÷ 10 =	44 ÷ 4 =	120 ÷ 10 =	36 ÷ 3 =	25 ÷ 5 =
66 ÷ 11 =	72 ÷ 8 =	36 ÷ 4 =	48 ÷ 6 =	24 ÷ 3 =
12 ÷ 4 =	18 ÷ 3 =	40 ÷ 10 =	18 ÷ 6 =	90 ÷ 9 =
121 ÷ 11 =	24 ÷ 6 =	30 ÷ 6 =	20 ÷ 5 =	88 ÷ 8 =
48 ÷ 12 =	40 ÷ 4 =	108 ÷ 9 =	60 ÷ 10 =	33 ÷ 11 =
60 ÷ 6 =	45 ÷ 9 =	56 ÷ 8 =	100 ÷ 10 =	144 ÷ 12 =
60 ÷ 12 =	21 ÷ 7 =	54 ÷ 9 =	48 ÷ 8 =	24 ÷ 4 =
132 ÷ 11 =	27 ÷ 9 =	28 ÷ 4 =	9 ÷ 3 =	84 ÷ 7 =
96 ÷ 8 =	72 ÷ 6 =	132 ÷ 12 =	66 ÷ 6 =	55 ÷ 11 =
36 ÷ 12 =	70 ÷ 7 =	40 ÷ 8 =	80 ÷ 8 =	99 ÷ 11 =

Name _____   Date _____

36 ÷ 12 =	90 ÷ 9 =	24 ÷ 4 =	50 ÷ 5 =	60 ÷ 12 =
20 ÷ 4 =	99 ÷ 11 =	100 ÷ 10 =	21 ÷ 7 =	33 ÷ 11 =
96 ÷ 8 =	55 ÷ 5 =	32 ÷ 4 =	45 ÷ 9 =	40 ÷ 5 =
99 ÷ 9 =	45 ÷ 5 =	9 ÷ 3 =	49 ÷ 7 =	12 ÷ 4 =
63 ÷ 7 =	24 ÷ 6 =	48 ÷ 8 =	54 ÷ 6 =	36 ÷ 9 =
72 ÷ 8 =	16 ÷ 4 =	81 ÷ 9 =	60 ÷ 10 =	96 ÷ 12 =
44 ÷ 11 =	21 ÷ 3 =	44 ÷ 4 =	35 ÷ 7 =	72 ÷ 12 =
24 ÷ 8 =	27 ÷ 9 =	110 ÷ 11 =	64 ÷ 8 =	56 ÷ 7 =
40 ÷ 10 =	66 ÷ 6 =	27 ÷ 3 =	72 ÷ 9 =	90 ÷ 10 =
84 ÷ 7 =	30 ÷ 3 =	48 ÷ 12 =	36 ÷ 3 =	30 ÷ 6 =
50 ÷ 10 =	88 ÷ 11 =	40 ÷ 4 =	30 ÷ 5 =	72 ÷ 6 =
60 ÷ 5 =	24 ÷ 3 =	77 ÷ 7 =	60 ÷ 6 =	32 ÷ 8 =
70 ÷ 10 =	144 ÷ 12 =	42 ÷ 6 =	80 ÷ 8 =	36 ÷ 4 =
108 ÷ 12 =	48 ÷ 4 =	56 ÷ 8 =	36 ÷ 6 =	120 ÷ 12 =
132 ÷ 11 =	70 ÷ 7 =	132 ÷ 12 =	28 ÷ 4 =	12 ÷ 3 =
42 ÷ 7 =	25 ÷ 5 =	18 ÷ 3 =	110 ÷ 10 =	18 ÷ 6 =
20 ÷ 5 =	84 ÷ 12 =	54 ÷ 9 =	33 ÷ 3 =	80 ÷ 10 =
35 ÷ 5 =	121 ÷ 11 =	48 ÷ 6 =	15 ÷ 5 =	77 ÷ 11 =
66 ÷ 11 =	63 ÷ 9 =	40 ÷ 8 =	15 ÷ 3 =	30 ÷ 10 =
28 ÷ 7 =	120 ÷ 10 =	55 ÷ 11 =	88 ÷ 8 =	108 ÷ 9 =

Name _____ Date _____

63 ÷ 9 =	16 ÷ 4 =	30 ÷ 6 =	48 ÷ 12 =	70 ÷ 7 =
44 ÷ 4 =	55 ÷ 11 =	60 ÷ 12 =	49 ÷ 7 =	25 ÷ 5 =
80 ÷ 10 =	70 ÷ 10 =	36 ÷ 12 =	96 ÷ 12 =	77 ÷ 11 =
36 ÷ 6 =	35 ÷ 7 =	35 ÷ 5 =	48 ÷ 6 =	30 ÷ 10 =
36 ÷ 9 =	72 ÷ 9 =	33 ÷ 11 =	88 ÷ 11 =	84 ÷ 7 =
40 ÷ 5 =	20 ÷ 5 =	50 ÷ 5 =	48 ÷ 4 =	72 ÷ 12 =
15 ÷ 5 =	42 ÷ 6 =	108 ÷ 9 =	21 ÷ 7 =	90 ÷ 9 =
66 ÷ 6 =	12 ÷ 4 =	45 ÷ 9 =	81 ÷ 9 =	40 ÷ 8 =
40 ÷ 4 =	40 ÷ 10 =	15 ÷ 3 =	72 ÷ 8 =	24 ÷ 8 =
18 ÷ 6 =	48 ÷ 8 =	28 ÷ 7 =	100 ÷ 10 =	56 ÷ 7 =
33 ÷ 3 =	9 ÷ 3 =	32 ÷ 8 =	24 ÷ 4 =	88 ÷ 8 =
72 ÷ 6 =	63 ÷ 7 =	27 ÷ 9 =	54 ÷ 6 =	27 ÷ 3 =
132 ÷ 11 =	32 ÷ 4 =	36 ÷ 3 =	28 ÷ 4 =	110 ÷ 10 =
110 ÷ 11 =	30 ÷ 3 =	54 ÷ 9 =	90 ÷ 10 =	44 ÷ 11 =
80 ÷ 8 =	12 ÷ 3 =	66 ÷ 11 =	84 ÷ 12 =	96 ÷ 8 =
60 ÷ 5 =	99 ÷ 11 =	20 ÷ 4 =	120 ÷ 12 =	64 ÷ 8 =
77 ÷ 7 =	24 ÷ 6 =	120 ÷ 10 =	21 ÷ 3 =	56 ÷ 8 =
132 ÷ 12 =	24 ÷ 3 =	30 ÷ 5 =	18 ÷ 3 =	121 ÷ 11 =
45 ÷ 5 =	60 ÷ 6 =	36 ÷ 4 =	99 ÷ 9 =	50 ÷ 10 =
55 ÷ 5 =	42 ÷ 7 =	144 ÷ 12 =	108 ÷ 12 =	60 ÷ 10 =

Name _____   Date _____

77 ÷ 7 =	48 ÷ 12 =	32 ÷ 8 =	12 ÷ 4 =	56 ÷ 7 =
55 ÷ 5 =	99 ÷ 9 =	16 ÷ 4 =	56 ÷ 8 =	48 ÷ 8 =
72 ÷ 6 =	50 ÷ 5 =	28 ÷ 7 =	35 ÷ 7 =	33 ÷ 11 =
25 ÷ 5 =	54 ÷ 9 =	40 ÷ 8 =	24 ÷ 4 =	36 ÷ 12 =
15 ÷ 5 =	64 ÷ 8 =	30 ÷ 6 =	49 ÷ 7 =	30 ÷ 5 =
70 ÷ 10 =	60 ÷ 5 =	24 ÷ 3 =	36 ÷ 9 =	90 ÷ 9 =
36 ÷ 4 =	40 ÷ 10 =	110 ÷ 10 =	80 ÷ 8 =	121 ÷ 11 =
88 ÷ 8 =	99 ÷ 11 =	72 ÷ 12 =	96 ÷ 8 =	63 ÷ 9 =
60 ÷ 10 =	42 ÷ 7 =	48 ÷ 4 =	32 ÷ 4 =	108 ÷ 9 =
20 ÷ 4 =	120 ÷ 12 =	27 ÷ 9 =	90 ÷ 10 =	45 ÷ 5 =
9 ÷ 3 =	18 ÷ 6 =	28 ÷ 4 =	24 ÷ 6 =	21 ÷ 7 =
44 ÷ 11 =	100 ÷ 10 =	66 ÷ 11 =	20 ÷ 5 =	70 ÷ 7 =
72 ÷ 8 =	30 ÷ 10 =	50 ÷ 10 =	120 ÷ 10 =	60 ÷ 12 =
40 ÷ 5 =	35 ÷ 5 =	55 ÷ 11 =	33 ÷ 3 =	110 ÷ 11 =
60 ÷ 6 =	84 ÷ 7 =	27 ÷ 3 =	144 ÷ 12 =	24 ÷ 8 =
36 ÷ 3 =	48 ÷ 6 =	84 ÷ 12 =	96 ÷ 12 =	42 ÷ 6 =
81 ÷ 9 =	132 ÷ 11 =	54 ÷ 6 =	88 ÷ 11 =	108 ÷ 12 =
36 ÷ 6 =	45 ÷ 9 =	66 ÷ 6 =	77 ÷ 11 =	30 ÷ 3 =
132 ÷ 12 =	72 ÷ 9 =	63 ÷ 7 =	12 ÷ 3 =	21 ÷ 3 =
18 ÷ 3 =	15 ÷ 3 =	40 ÷ 4 =	44 ÷ 4 =	80 ÷ 10 =

Name _____ Date _____

50 ÷ 5 =	48 ÷ 12 =	24 ÷ 8 =	56 ÷ 7 =	42 ÷ 6 =
12 ÷ 3 =	60 ÷ 12 =	110 ÷ 10 =	15 ÷ 5 =	44 ÷ 11 =
21 ÷ 7 =	54 ÷ 6 =	36 ÷ 9 =	77 ÷ 7 =	21 ÷ 3 =
90 ÷ 10 =	66 ÷ 6 =	45 ÷ 9 =	81 ÷ 9 =	30 ÷ 6 =
144 ÷ 12 =	70 ÷ 10 =	72 ÷ 6 =	40 ÷ 8 =	72 ÷ 9 =
132 ÷ 12 =	72 ÷ 8 =	15 ÷ 3 =	100 ÷ 10 =	36 ÷ 6 =
80 ÷ 10 =	24 ÷ 6 =	44 ÷ 4 =	12 ÷ 4 =	70 ÷ 7 =
42 ÷ 7 =	33 ÷ 3 =	108 ÷ 12 =	30 ÷ 5 =	60 ÷ 5 =
56 ÷ 8 =	45 ÷ 5 =	110 ÷ 11 =	40 ÷ 4 =	77 ÷ 11 =
9 ÷ 3 =	60 ÷ 6 =	96 ÷ 12 =	20 ÷ 5 =	24 ÷ 4 =
36 ÷ 12 =	48 ÷ 6 =	64 ÷ 8 =	50 ÷ 10 =	99 ÷ 11 =
55 ÷ 5 =	35 ÷ 7 =	88 ÷ 11 =	132 ÷ 11 =	36 ÷ 3 =
18 ÷ 6 =	55 ÷ 11 =	40 ÷ 10 =	66 ÷ 11 =	121 ÷ 11 =
32 ÷ 8 =	30 ÷ 3 =	16 ÷ 4 =	72 ÷ 12 =	33 ÷ 11 =
27 ÷ 3 =	80 ÷ 8 =	18 ÷ 3 =	99 ÷ 9 =	40 ÷ 5 =
25 ÷ 5 =	63 ÷ 7 =	36 ÷ 4 =	35 ÷ 5 =	30 ÷ 10 =
32 ÷ 4 =	49 ÷ 7 =	63 ÷ 9 =	84 ÷ 7 =	120 ÷ 10 =
96 ÷ 8 =	48 ÷ 8 =	28 ÷ 4 =	60 ÷ 10 =	27 ÷ 9 =
20 ÷ 4 =	84 ÷ 12 =	108 ÷ 9 =	120 ÷ 12 =	48 ÷ 4 =
90 ÷ 9 =	28 ÷ 7 =	88 ÷ 8 =	54 ÷ 9 =	24 ÷ 3 =

Name _____   Date _____

84 ÷ 12 =	70 ÷ 10 =	63 ÷ 9 =	24 ÷ 8 =	48 ÷ 12 =
16 ÷ 4 =	32 ÷ 4 =	100 ÷ 10 =	60 ÷ 12 =	18 ÷ 6 =
49 ÷ 7 =	24 ÷ 3 =	56 ÷ 7 =	96 ÷ 12 =	63 ÷ 7 =
32 ÷ 8 =	27 ÷ 3 =	50 ÷ 5 =	80 ÷ 10 =	30 ÷ 5 =
120 ÷ 10 =	35 ÷ 5 =	21 ÷ 3 =	80 ÷ 8 =	48 ÷ 8 =
9 ÷ 3 =	60 ÷ 5 =	45 ÷ 5 =	132 ÷ 12 =	55 ÷ 5 =
132 ÷ 11 =	81 ÷ 9 =	99 ÷ 11 =	55 ÷ 11 =	25 ÷ 5 =
50 ÷ 10 =	20 ÷ 5 =	48 ÷ 6 =	77 ÷ 7 =	42 ÷ 7 =
24 ÷ 4 =	12 ÷ 4 =	20 ÷ 4 =	15 ÷ 3 =	77 ÷ 11 =
121 ÷ 11 =	88 ÷ 11 =	66 ÷ 11 =	64 ÷ 8 =	36 ÷ 4 =
12 ÷ 3 =	72 ÷ 8 =	60 ÷ 10 =	56 ÷ 8 =	144 ÷ 12 =
45 ÷ 9 =	88 ÷ 8 =	40 ÷ 8 =	40 ÷ 10 =	33 ÷ 3 =
28 ÷ 7 =	36 ÷ 9 =	36 ÷ 12 =	42 ÷ 6 =	54 ÷ 9 =
30 ÷ 6 =	30 ÷ 10 =	21 ÷ 7 =	110 ÷ 10 =	24 ÷ 6 =
54 ÷ 6 =	40 ÷ 5 =	99 ÷ 9 =	28 ÷ 4 =	44 ÷ 4 =
30 ÷ 3 =	90 ÷ 10 =	110 ÷ 11 =	84 ÷ 7 =	27 ÷ 9 =
90 ÷ 9 =	33 ÷ 11 =	72 ÷ 9 =	72 ÷ 6 =	15 ÷ 5 =
36 ÷ 3 =	66 ÷ 6 =	40 ÷ 4 =	120 ÷ 12 =	60 ÷ 6 =
18 ÷ 3 =	96 ÷ 8 =	108 ÷ 12 =	70 ÷ 7 =	35 ÷ 7 =
72 ÷ 12 =	36 ÷ 6 =	44 ÷ 11 =	108 ÷ 9 =	48 ÷ 4 =

MATH WORKBOOK
5 MINUTE DRILLS
ADDITION, SUBTRACTION
MULTIPLICATION, DIVISION

100 WORKSHEETS

Copyright © 2020

Made in the USA
Columbia, SC
09 March 2022